BUS

ALLEN COUNTY PUBLIC LIBRARY

P9-AFY-504

BLACK & DECKER ®
HOME IMPROVEMENT LIBRARY™

Sheds,
Gazebos & Outbuildings

8 Projects with
Plans & Instructions

by
Philip Schmidt

CREATIVE
PUBLISHING
international

MINNETONKA, MINNESOTA

www.creativepub.com

© Copyright 2002
Creative Publishing international, Inc.
5900 Green Oak Drive
Minnetonka, Minnesota 55343
1-800-328-3895
www.creativepub.com
All rights reserved

Printed by R.R. Donnelly & Sons Co.
10 9 8 7 6 5 4 3 2 1

President/CEO: Michael Eleftheriou
Vice President/Publisher: Linda Ball
Vice President/Retail Sales & Marketing: Kevin Haas

Executive Editor: Bryan Trandem
Creative Director: Tim Himsel
Managing Editor: Michelle Skudlarek
Editorial Director: Jerri Farris

Author: Philip Schmidt
Senior Art Director: David Schelitzche
Copy Editors: Barbara Harold, Tracy Stanley
Technical Photo Editor: Paul Gorton
Illustrators: Jan Boer, Patti Goar, Wayne Jeske, Melanie Powell,
   David Schelitzche, Jon Simpson
Photo Editor: Angela Hartwell
Studio Services Manager: Marcia Chambers
Photographers: Tate Carlson, Andrea Rugg
Scene Shop Carpenters: Scott Ashfield, Dan Widerski
Director of Production Services: Kim Gerber
Production Manager: Helga Thielen

SHEDS, GAZEBOS & OUTBUILDINGS
Created by: The Editors of Creative Publishing international, Inc.,
in cooperation with Black & Decker. Black & Decker® is a trademark of
The Black & Decker Corporation and is used under license.

Library of Congress

Cataloging-in-Publication Data
Sheds, gazebos & outbuildings: complete plans and instructions for 8 projects.
        p. cm. – (Black & Decker home improvement library)
     Includes index.
     ISBN 1-58923-008-6 (softcover)
        1. Toolsheds–Design and construction–Amateurs' manuals.
     2. Sheds–Design and constraction–Amateurs' manuals. 3. Gazebos–Design
     and construction–Amateurs' manuals. 4. Outbuildings–Design and
     construction–Amateurs' manuals. 5. Garden structures–Designs and
     plans–Amateurs' manuals. I. Title: Sheds, gazebos, and outbuildings.
     II. Creative Publishing International. III. Series.

TH4962 .S54 2001
690'.89–dc21
                                                        2001055521

Other titles from Creative Publishing international include:
*New Everyday Home Repairs, Basic Wiring & Electrical Repairs, Advanced
Home Wiring, Landscape Design & Construction, Bathroom Remodeling,
Built-In Projects for the Home, Refinishing & Finishing Wood, Home
Masonry Repairs & Projects, Building Porches & Patios, Flooring Projects
& Techniques, Advanced Home Plumbing, Remodeling Kitchens, Stonework
& Masonry Projects, Finishing Basements & Attics, Carpentry:
Remodeling, Carpentry: Tools•Walls•Shelves•Doors, Great Decks, Building
Decks, Advanced Deck Building, The Complete Guide to Home Plumbing,
The Complete Guide to Home Wiring, The Complete Guide to Building
Decks, The Complete Guide to Painting & Decorating, The Complete Guide
to Creative Landscapes, The Complete Guide to Home Masonry, The
Complete Guide to Home Carpentry, The Complete Guide to Home Storage,
The Complete Photo Guide to Home Repair, The Complete Photo Guide to
Home Improvement*

Contents

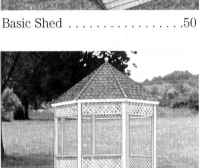

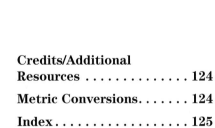
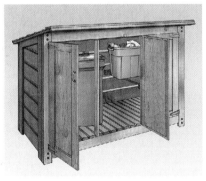

NOTICE TO READERS

This book provides useful instructions, but we cannot anticipate all of your working conditions or the characteristics of your materials and tools. For safety, you should use caution, care, and good judgment when following the procedures described in this book. Consider your own skill level and the instructions and safety precautions associated with the various tools and materials shown. Neither the publisher nor Black & Decker® can assume responsibility for any damage to property or injury to persons as a result of misuse of the information provided.

Introduction

Constructing your own outbuilding is a satisfying process—from hand-picking the lumber to poring over the plans to nailing off the final piece of trim. In the end, you'll have a well-built, custom structure that will far outlast any typical wood or sheet metal kit building. And if you're a beginner, you'll enjoy the added reward of learning the fundamentals of carpentry and building design.

In many ways, outbuildings—especially sheds—are like little houses and have many of the same design elements and materials. A good outbuilding doesn't have to look like a house (that would be an odd requirement for a gazebo), but it should include architectural details that fit the proportions and overall style of the building—that is, it should be a building unto itself, and not just a storage box with a roof and a padlock on the door.

All of the building projects in this book accomplish that basic design goal. Elements such as size, shape, and roof frame, as well as exterior finishes and trim, were chosen to match the practical nature and character of each building. But that doesn't mean you have to follow the plans entirely. You may decide, for example, to use cedar siding instead of grooved plywood, or metal roofing rather than asphalt shingles. For help with these decisions, look to the reference section, Building Materials & Techniques, starting on page 9.

In addition to showing the most popular types of finishes and how to apply them, the Techniques section teaches you the basic construction skills needed to complete the projects in the book. You'll learn how to build foundations, lay out walls, cut rafters, sheath roofs, even hang doors. Not all of the procedures apply to every project, but you'll find helpful principles throughout the section, regardless of what you're building. It's important to note that the step-by-step instructions for each of the projects follow the building process from beginning to end, but in a somewhat abbreviated form. If you need more detail on any of the procedures, look for it in the Techniques section.

When you're ready to start planning, be sure you've read Choosing the Site, on page 6. This includes tips for selecting the best area for your outbuilding and a discussion of the legal issues that may apply to your project—namely, building codes and zoning regulations. Depending on a few factors, such as the type of building and its foundation, and where you live, you may have to gain approval for your project before you begin.

Photo courtesy of Gardensheds

4

Choosing the Site

The first step in choosing a site for your building doesn't take place in your backyard but at the local building and zoning departments. By visiting the departments, or making calls, you should determine a few things about your project before making any definite plans. Most importantly, find out whether your proposed building will be allowed by zoning regulations and what specific restrictions apply to your situation. Zoning laws govern such matters as the size and height of the building and the percentage of your property it occupies, the building's location, and its position relative to the house, neighboring properties, the street, etc.

From the building side of things, ask if you need a permit to build your structure. If so, you'll have to submit plan drawings (this book should suffice), as well as specifications for the foundation and materials. Once your project is approved, you must buy a permit to display on the building site, and you may be required to show your work at scheduled inspections.

Because outbuildings are by nature detached and freestanding, building codes typically govern them much more loosely than they do houses. Many impose restrictions or require permits only on structures larger than 100, or even 120, square feet. Others draw the line with the type of foundation used. In some areas, buildings with concrete slab or pier foundations are classified as "permanent" and thus are subject to a specific set of restrictions (and taxation, in some cases), while buildings that are set on skids and can—in theory at least—be moved are considered temporary or accessory and may be exempt from the general building codes. Again, municipal laws vary greatly, so you'll have to find out which ones apply to you.

Once you get the green light from the local authorities, you can tromp around your yard with a tape measure and stake your claim for the new building. Of course, you'll have plenty of personal and practical reasons for placing the building in a particular area, but here are a few general considerations to keep in mind:

Sunlight: How much light you want will depend on the building's purpose. South-facing windows and doors bring in the most sunlight; a playhouse or gazebo may benefit from some shading. Also consider what the building itself will shade, lest you block essential light to your garden.

Soil & drainage: To ensure that your foundation will last (whatever type it is), plant your building on solid soil, in an area that won't collect water.

Access: For trucks, wheelbarrows, kids, etc. Do you want access in all seasons?

Utility lines: Contact the local utilities to find out where the water, gas, and electrical lines run through your property. This is essential not only for digging in the ground, but also because you don't want your building sitting over lines that may need repair.

Setback requirements: Most zoning laws dictate that all buildings, fences, etc., in a yard must be set back a specific distance from the property line. This *setback* may range from 6" to 3 ft. or more.

Neighbors: To prevent civil unrest, or even a few weeks of ignored greetings, talk to your neighbors about your project.

View from the house: Do you want to admire you handiwork from the dinner table, or would you prefer that your outbuilding blend in with the outdoors? A playhouse in plain view makes it easy to check on the kids.

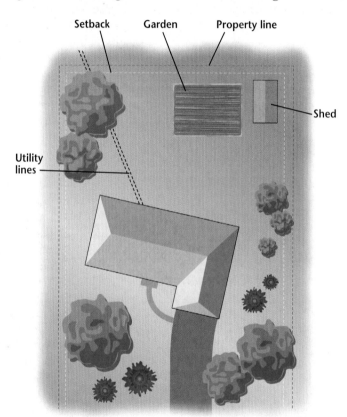

Setback   Garden   Property line

Utility lines

Shed

Working with Plans

Architectural plan drawings are two-dimensional representations of what a building looks like from five different perspectives, or *views*: front, rear, right side, left side, and plan view. The first four are called ELEVATIONS, and they show you what you would see with a direct, exterior view of the building. There are elevation drawings for the framing and for the exterior finishes. PLAN views have an overhead perspective, looking straight down from above the building. FLOOR PLANS show the wall layout, with the top half of the building sliced off. There are also roof framing plans and other drawings with plan views.

To show close-up views of specific constructions or relationships between materials, there are various DETAILS. And all plans include a comprehensive building SECTION—a side view of the building sliced in half down the middle, showing both the framing and finish elements.

Because plan drawings are two-dimensional, it's up to you to visualize the building in its actual, three-dimensional form. This can be done by cross-referencing the different drawings and confirming the quantities and sizes of materials using the materials list. It helps to spend some time just looking over the drawings. Chances are, you'll find yourself absorbed in solving the puzzle of how it all fits together.

Note: the plan drawings in this book are not sized to a specific scale, but all of the elements within each drawing are sized proportionately. And although the plan dimensions are given in feet and inches (6'-8", for example), the instructions provide dimensions in inches, so you don't have to make the conversion.

Here are some of the common terms and conventions used in the drawings in this book:

- **Wall height** is measured from the top of the finished floor to the top of the wall framing.

- **Rough openings** for doors and windows are measured between the framing members inside the opening. An opening's width and height are given on separate drawings.

- **Grade** represents the solid, level ground directly beneath the building.

- **Door & window details** typically show a gap between the 1 × frame and the framing of the rough opening—this represents the shim space needed for installing the frames using shims.

- **Framing layout** is noted with a dimension (usually 16" or 24"), followed by "on center" or "O. C." This describes the spacing between the center of one framing member to the center of the next member. Use the spacing for the general layout, adding extra members, such as for corners and door or window frames, where noted. The last space in a layout is often smaller than the given on-center dimension.

BUILDING SECTION

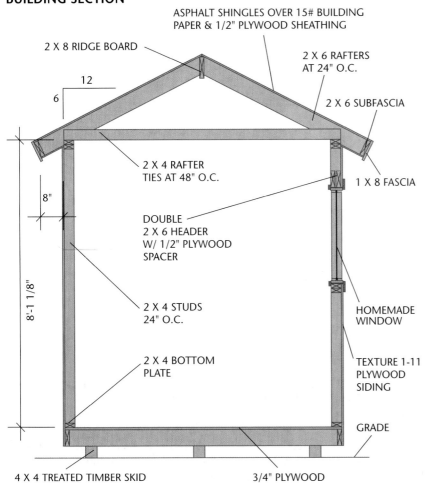

ASPHALT SHINGLES OVER 15# BUILDING PAPER & 1/2" PLYWOOD SHEATHING

2 X 8 RIDGE BOARD

2 X 6 RAFTERS AT 24" O.C.

2 X 6 SUBFASCIA

12

6

2 X 4 RAFTER TIES AT 48" O.C.

1 X 8 FASCIA

DOUBLE 2 X 6 HEADER W/ 1/2" PLYWOOD SPACER

8"

2 X 4 STUDS 24" O.C.

HOMEMADE WINDOW

8'-1 1/8"

2 X 4 BOTTOM PLATE

TEXTURE 1-11 PLYWOOD SIDING

GRADE

4 X 4 TREATED TIMBER SKID

3/4" PLYWOOD

Building Materials & Techniques

Building Anatomy

Shown as a cutaway, this shed illustrates many of the standard building components and how they fit together. It can also help you understand the major construction stages—each project in this book includes a specific construction sequence, but most follow the standard stages in some form:

1. Foundation—including preparing the site and adding a drainage bed; 2. Framing—the floor is first, followed by the walls, then the roof; 3. Roofing—adding sheathing, building paper, and roofing material; 4. Exterior finishes—including siding, trim, and doors and windows.

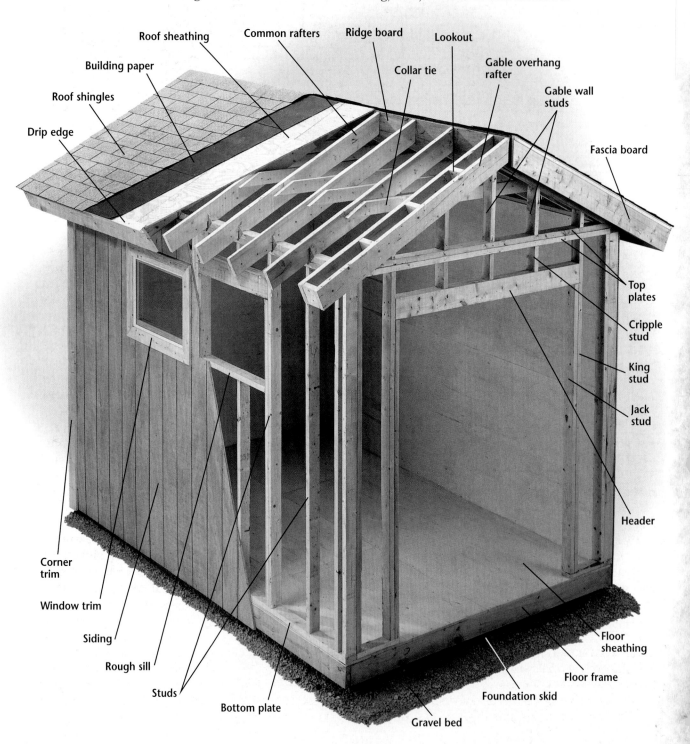

Roof sheathing

Common rafters

Ridge board

Lookout

Building paper

Collar tie

Gable overhang rafter

Roof shingles

Gable wall studs

Drip edge

Fascia board

Top plates

Cripple stud

King stud

Jack stud

Header

Corner trim

Window trim

Siding

Rough sill

Studs

Bottom plate

Floor sheathing

Floor frame

Foundation skid

Gravel bed

Lumber & Hardware

Lumber types most commonly used in outbuildings are pine—or related softwoods—or cedar, which is naturally rot-resistant and is less expensive than most other rot-resistant woods. For pine to be rot-resistant, it must be pressure-treated, typically with a chemical mixture called CCA (Chromated Copper Arsenate).

texture. S4S (Surfaced-Four-Sides) cedar is milled smooth on all sides and follows the standard dimensioning, while boards with one or more rough surfaces can be over ⅛" thicker.

When selecting hardware for your project, remember one thing: all nails, screws, bolts, hinges, or anchors that will be exposed to water or rest on concrete must be galvanized or made of a rust-resistant metal, such as aluminum or stainless steel. Other protective coatings exist, but galvanized hardware is the most common and usually the least expensive. A note about cedar: when exposed, galvanized fasteners can cause staining on cedar. The only sure bet against staining (and corrosion) is stainless steel—a pricey option.

Pressure-treated lumber is cheaper than cedar, but it's not as attractive, so you may want to use it only in areas where appearance is unimportant. Plywood designated as exterior-grade is made with layers of cedar or treated wood and a special glue that makes it weather-resistant. For the long run, though, it's a good idea to cover any exposed plywood edges to prevent water intrusion.

Framing lumber—typically pine or pressure-treated pine—comes in a few different grades: Select Structural (SEL STR), Construction (CONST) or Standard (STAND), and Utility (UTIL). For most applications, Construction Grade No. 2 offers the best balance between quality and price. Utility grade is a lower-cost lumber suitable for blocking and similar uses but should not be used for structural members, such as studs and rafters. You can also buy "STUD" lumber: construction-grade 2 × 4s cut at the standard stud length of 92⅝".

Board lumber, or *finish* lumber, is graded by quality and appearance, with the main criteria being the number and size of knots present. "Clear" pine, for example, has no knots.

All lumber has a nominal dimension (what it's called) and an actual dimension (what it actually measures), and the two are seldom the same. A chart on page 124 shows the differences for some common lumber sizes. Lumber that is greater than 4" thick (nominally) generally is referred to as *timber*. Depending on its surface texture and type, a timber may actually measure to its nominal dimensions, so check this out before buying. Cedar lumber also varies in size, depending on its surface

Another type of hardware you'll find throughout this book is the metal anchor, used to reinforce framing connections. All of the anchors called for in the plans are Simpson Strong-Tie® brand, which are commonly available at lumberyards and home centers. If you can't find what you need on the shelves, look through one of the manufacturer's catalogs or visit their website (see page 124). You can also order custom-made hangers. Keep in mind that metal anchors are effective only if they are installed correctly—always follow the manufacturer's installation instructions, and use exactly the type and number of fastener recommended.

Finally, applying a finish to your project will help protect the wood from rot, fading and discoloration, and insects. Pine or similar untreated lumber must have a protective finish if it's exposed to the elements, but even cedar is susceptible to rot over time and will turn gray if left bare. If you paint the wood, apply a primer first—this helps the paint stick and makes it last longer. If you want to preserve the natural wood grain, use a stain or clear finish. Because weather and available wood species vary by region, ask at the lumberyard for the best products to use on your lumber.

Foundations

Like a house, a shed or gazebo needs a foundation to provide a sturdy base to build upon and to protect the structure from the damaging effects of moisture and soil. In some cases the foundation ties the building to the earth (an important requirement for umbrella-like gazebos) or keeps the building from shifting during seasonal freeze-thaw cycles.

You can build a shed with a variety of foundations; the most commonly used types are the wooden skid and the concrete slab. In addition to being far easier and cheaper to construct, a skid foundation allows you to move the shed if you need to. It also ensures—in most areas—that the building is classified as a temporary structure (see page 6). A

concrete slab, by contrast, gives you a nice, hard-wearing floor as well as an extremely durable foundation. But a concrete foundation means the building is considered "permanent," which could affect the tax assessment of your property; you'll also most likely need a permit for the project.

Gazebos must be securely anchored to the ground, as mentioned, and are typically built on concrete pier or slab foundations. For very small projects you probably won't need a foundation—just make sure the base or posts that sit on the ground are made of rot-resistant lumber.

Wooden Skid Foundation

A skid foundation couldn't be simpler: two or more treated wood beams or landscape timbers (typically 4×4, 4×6, or 6×6) set on a bed of gravel. The gravel provides a flat, stable surface that drains well to help keep the timbers dry. Once the skids are set, the floor frame is built on top of them and is nailed to the skids to keep everything in place.

Building a skid foundation is merely a matter of preparing the gravel base, then cutting, setting, and leveling the timbers. The timbers you use must be rated for ground contact. It is customary, but purely optional, to make angled cuts on the ends of the skids—these add a minor decorative touch and make it easier to *skid* the shed to a new location, if necessary.

Because a skid foundation sits on the ground, it is subject to slight shifting due to frost in cold-weather climates. Often a shed that has risen out of level will correct itself with the spring thaw, but if it doesn't, you can lift the shed with jacks on the low side and add gravel beneath the skids to level it.

TOOLS & MATERIALS

Shovel	Circular saw
Rake	Square
4-ft. level	Treated wood timbers
Straight, 8-ft. 2 x 4	Compactible gravel
Hand tamper	Wood sealer-preservative

A. *Excavate the building site and add a 4" layer of compactible gravel. Level, then tamp the gravel with a hand tamper or rented plate compactor (inset).*

HOW TO BUILD A WOODEN SKID FOUNDATION
Step A: Prepare the Gravel Base

1. Remove 4" of soil in an area about 12" wider and longer than the dimensions of the building.

2. Fill the excavated area with a 4" layer of compactible gravel. Rake the gravel smooth, then check it for level using a 4-ft. level and a straight, 8-ft.-long 2 × 4. Rake the gravel until it is fairly level.

3. Tamp the gravel thoroughly using a hand tamper or a rented plate compactor. As you work, check the surface with the board and level, and add or remove gravel until the surface is level.

Step B: Cut & Set the Skids

1. Cut the skids to length, using a circular saw or reciprocating saw. (Skids typically run parallel to the length of the building and are cut to the same dimension as the floor frame.)

2. To angle-cut the ends, measure down 1½" to 2" from the top edge of each skid. Use a square to mark a 45° cutting line down to the bottom edge, then make the cuts.

3. Coat the cut ends of the skids with a wood sealer-preservative and let them dry.

4. Set the skids on the gravel so they are parallel and their ends are even. Make sure the outer skids are spaced according to the width of the building.

Step C: Level the Skids

1. Level one of the outside skids, adding or removing gravel from underneath. Set the level parallel and level the skid along its length, then set the level perpendicular and level the skid along its width.

2. Place the straight 2 × 4 and level across the first and second skids, then adjust the second skid until it's level with the first. Make sure the second skid is level along its width.

3. Level the remaining skids in the same fashion, then set the board and level across all of the skids to make sure they they are level with one another.

B. *If desired, mark and clip the bottom corners of the skid ends. Use a square to mark a 45° angle cut.*

C. *Using a board and a level, make sure each skid is level along its width and length, and is level with the other skids.*

Concrete Pier Foundation

A concrete pier foundation consists of poured-concrete cylinders that support wood posts. The piers, or *footings*, are the same as those used for deck construction. They are easy to make using cardboard forms that you cut to size.

To anchor the posts to the footings, it's best to use galvanized metal post bases. There are several easy-to-use adjustable types available, which are secured to the footing by means of a J-bolt set into the concrete. After the concrete is dry, you bolt down the base, set and plumb the post, and fasten the post to the base.

Pier foundations work well for gazebos because they allow you to build an elevated floor while keeping the structure securely planted in the earth. For sheds, piers offer a permanently fixed foundation and protection against frost heaves. If you're building a shed on level ground, use pads made from pressure-treated 2 × lumber instead of posts. Anchor the pads to the piers using the J-bolts, and build the floor frame on top of the pads.

Constructing a pier foundation is not difficult work, but it's important that the pier layout is accurate and the

concrete forms are set properly. Use batter boards and mason's lines to lay out the pier positions and check your work by taking measurements and applying some simple geometry.

Before starting your project, ask the local building department about the required diameter and depth of your piers and what type of post anchors to use. In most areas, concrete piers must extend into the ground below the frost line and stand at least 2" above the ground to protect the posts from moisture. Cardboard forms for piers are commonly available in 8", 10", 12", and 16" diameters.

TOOLS & MATERIALS

Circular saw	2½" screws
Drill	Stakes
Mason's line	Nails
Sledgehammer	Masking tape
Line level	Cardboard concrete forms
Framing square	Paper
Plumb bob	Concrete mix
Shovel	J-bolts
Post hole digger	Post bases
Reciprocating saw or handsaw	Straight board
Utility knife	Wood sealer-preservative
Ratchet wrench	Scrap lumber for braces
2 x 4 lumber	Lag screws

HOW TO BUILD A CONCRETE PIER FOUNDATION

Step A: Construct the Batter Boards

1. Cut two 24"- long 2 × 4 legs for each batter board (for most projects you'll need eight batter boards total). Cut one end square and cut the other end to a sharp point, using a circular saw. Cut one 2 × 4 crosspiece for each batter board at about 18".

2. Assemble each batter board using 2½" screws. Fasten the crosspiece about 2" from the square ends of the legs. Make sure the legs are parallel and the crosspiece is perpendicular to the legs.

Step B: Set the Batter Boards & Establish Perpendicular Mason's Lines

1. Measure and mark the locations of the piers with stakes, following your project plan.

2. Set two batter boards to form a corner about 18" behind each stake, as shown in the illustration on page 15. Drive the batter boards into the ground until they are secure, keeping the crosspieces roughly level with one another.

3. Stretch a mason's line between two batter

boards at opposing corners (not diagonally) and tie the ends to nails driven into the top edge of the crosspieces; align the nails and line with the stakes. Attach a line level to the line, and pull the line very taut, making sure it's level before tying it.

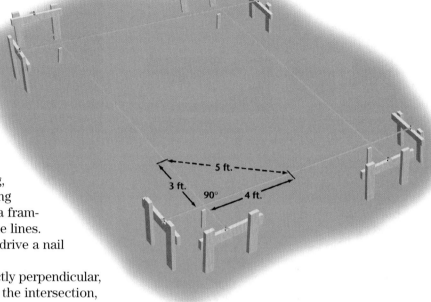

4. Run a second level line perpendicular to the first: Tie off the end that's closest to the first string, then stretch the line to the opposing batter board while a helper holds a framing square at the intersection of the lines. When the lines are perpendicular, drive a nail and tie off the far end.

5. Confirm that the lines are exactly perpendicular, using the 3-4-5 method. Starting at the intersection, measure 3 ft. along one string and make a mark onto a piece of masking tape. Mark the other string 4 ft. from the intersection. Measure diagonally between the two marks; the distance should equal 5 ft. Reposition the second string, if necessary, until the diagonal measurement is 5 ft.

Step C: Mark the Footing Locations

1. Following your plan, measure from the existing lines and use the 3-4-5 method to add two more perpendicular lines to form a layout with four 90° corners. Use the line level to make sure the mason's lines are level. The intersections of the lines should

mark the centers of the piers.

2. Check the squareness of your line layout by measuring diagonally from corner to corner: when the measurements are equal, the frame is square. Make any necessary adjustments.

3. Plumb down with a plumb bob and place a stake directly under each line intersection. If your plan calls for additional piers, as in the Gazebo project, measure and mark those points on the lines, then plumb down and plant the stakes.

4. Untie each line at one end only, then coil the

A. Cut the batter board pieces from 2 × 4 lumber and assemble them with screws.

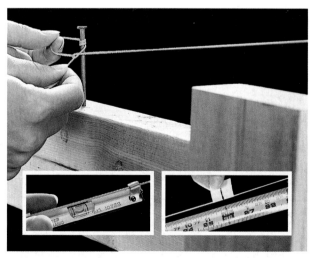

B. Tie the mason's lines securely to the nails, and level the lines with a line level (inset, left). Use tape to mark points on the lines (inset, right).

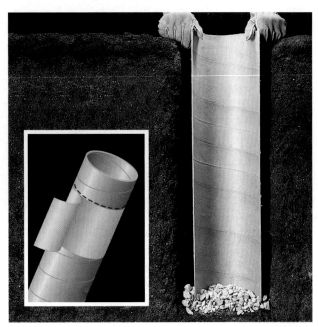

C. *Use a plumb bob to mark the pier locations. Drive a stake into the ground directly below the plumb bob pointer.*

D. *Wrap paper around the form to mark a straight cutting line (inset). Set the forms in the holes on top of a 4" gravel layer.*

line and place it out of the way. Leaving one end tied will make it easier to restring the lines later.

Step D: Set the Forms

1. Dig holes for the forms, centering them around the stakes. Make the holes a few inches larger in diameter than the cardboard forms. The hole depth must meet the local building code requirements—add 4" to the depth to allow for a layer of gravel. For deep holes, use a post hole digger or a rented power auger. Add 4" of gravel to the bottom of each hole.

2. Cut each cardboard form so it will extend 2" above the ground level. The top ends of the forms must be straight, so place the factory-cut end up, whenever possible. Otherwise, mark a straight cutting line using a large piece of paper with at least one straight edge: Wrap the paper completely around the form so that it overlaps itself a few inches. Position the straight edge of the paper on the cutting mark, and align the overlapping edges of the paper with each other. Mark around the tube along the edge of the paper. Cut the tube with a reciprocating saw or handsaw.

3. Set the tubes in the holes and fill in around them with dirt. Set a level across the top of each tube to make sure the top is level as you secure the tube with dirt. Pack the dirt firmly, using a shovel handle or a stick.

Step E: Pour the Concrete

1. Restring the mason's lines and confirm that the forms are positioned accurately.

2. Mix the concrete following the manufacturer's directions; prepare only as much as you can easily work with before the concrete sets. Fill each form with concrete, using a long stick to tamp it down and eliminate air pockets in the concrete. Overfill the form slightly.

3. Level the concrete by pulling a 2 × 4 on edge across the top of the form, using a side-to-side sawing motion. Fill low spots with concrete so that the top is perfectly flat.

4. Set a J-bolt into the wet concrete in the center of the form. Lower the bolt slowly, wiggling it slightly to eliminate air pockets. Use a plumb bob to make sure the bolt is aligned exactly with the mark on the mason's line. Make sure the bolt is plumb and extends ¾" to 1" above the concrete. Smooth the concrete around the bolt and let the concrete cure.

Step F: Install the Post Bases

1. Mark a reference line on the top of each pier to help with aligning the post bases. Place a long, straight board across two piers, setting it on the same side of each J-bolt. Hold the board against the bolts and trace along the edge (bolt-side) of the board onto the tops of the piers.

E. *Fill the forms with concrete, then set the J-bolts. Check with a plumb bob to make sure the bolts are centered.*

F. *Set the post base over the J-bolt and use a framing square and reference line to position the base before securing it.*

Note: If your footing layout is square or rectangular, make reference marks that follow the perimeter of the building. If you're building a gazebo, set the board across the center pier and each of the outside piers.

2. Place a post base on each pier so it's centered over the J-bolt. Add the washers and loosely screw the anchor nut onto the J-bolt. Use a framing square to position the base square with the reference line, then tighten the nut with a ratchet wrench.

3. Place the metal pedestals into the post bases.

Step G: Set the Posts

1. Make sure the bottom post ends are square; cut them, if necessary. Seal the bottom ends with a wood sealer-preservative, to prevent rot.

2. Place each post in its base, hold it plumb, and tack in one 16d galvanized common nail. Have a helper set up two perpendicular cross braces. Use a level to plumb the post, and secure the braces to the post and to stakes in the ground, using screws. Hold the level on two adjacent post faces to make sure the post is perfectly plumb. Nail the post to the base with 16d nails.

3. Drill pilot holes for the lag screws that anchor the posts to the bases (check with the manufacturer for the recommended size of lag screw). Install the lag screws with a ratchet wrench. Leave the

G. *Plumb and brace the posts, then secure the posts to the bases with galvanized nails and lag screws.*

braces in place until the top post ends are securely framed into the structure. Cut away the exposed portions of the forms with a utility knife.

Concrete Slab Foundation

The slab foundation commonly used for sheds is called a *slab-on-grade* foundation. This combines a 3½"- to 4"-thick floor slab with a 8"- to 12"-thick perimeter footing that provides extra support for the walls of the building. The whole foundation can be poured at one time using a simple wood form.

Because they sit above ground, slab-on-grade foundations are susceptible to frost heave and in cold-weather climates are suitable only for detached buildings. Specific design requirements also vary by locality, so check with the local building department regarding the depth of the slab, the metal reinforcement required, the type and amount of gravel required for the subbase, and whether plastic or an other type of moisture barrier is needed under the slab.

The slab shown in this project has a 3½"-thick interior with a 8"-wide × 8"-deep footing along the perimeter. The top of the slab sits 4" above ground level, or *grade*. There is a 4"-thick layer of compacted gravel underneath the slab and the concrete is reinforced internally with a layer of 6 × 6" 10/10 welded wire mesh (WWM). (In some areas, you may be required to add rebar in the foundation perimeter—check the local code.) After the concrete is poured and finished, 8"-long J-bolts are set into the slab along the edges. These are used later to anchor the wall framing to the slab.

A slab for a shed requires a lot of concrete: an 8 × 10-ft. slab designed like the one in this project calls for about 1.3 cubic yards of concrete; a 12 × 12-ft. slab, about 2.3 cubic yards (see ***Estimating Concrete***, on page 21). Considering the amount involved, you'll probably want to order ready-mix concrete delivered by truck to the site (most companies have a one-yard minimum). Order *air-entrained* concrete, which will hold up best, and tell the mixing company that you're using it for an exterior slab.

An alternative for smaller slabs is to rent a concrete trailer from a rental center or landscaping company; they fill the trailer with one yard of mixed concrete and you tow it home with your own vehicle.

If you're having your concrete delivered, be sure to have a few helpers on-hand when the truck arrives; neither the concrete nor the driver will wait for you to get organized. Also, concrete trucks must be unloaded completely, so designate a dumping spot for any excess. Once the form is filled, load a couple of wheelbarrows with concrete (in case you need it) then have the driver dump the rest. Be sure to spread out and hose down the excess concrete so you aren't left with an immovable boulder in your yard.

If you've never worked with concrete, finishing a large slab can be a challenging introduction; you might want some experienced help with the pour.

TOOLS & MATERIALS

Circular saw	Hand-held concrete float
Drill	Concrete edger
Mason's line	Compactible gravel
Sledgehammer	2 x 3 & 2 x 4 lumber
Line level	1¼" & 2½" deck screws
Framing square	¾" A-C plywood
Shovel	8d nails
Wheelbarrow	6 x 6" 10/10 welded wire mesh
Rented plate compactor	1½" brick pavers
Bolt cutters	J-bolts
Bull float	2"-thick rigid foam insulation

8"-thick perimeter

4" compacted gravel

Plywood form

Trench sloped 45°

Welded wire mesh

3½"-thick slab

HOW TO BUILD A CONCRETE SLAB FOUNDATION

Step A: Excavate the Site

1. Set up batter boards and run level mason's lines to represent the outer dimensions of the slab (see pages 14 to 16). Use the 3-4-5 method to make sure your lines are perpendicular, and check your final layout for squareness by measuring the diagonals.

2. Excavate the area 4" wider and longer than the string layout—this provides some room to work. For the footing portion along the perimeter, dig a trench that is 8" wide × 8" deep.

3. Remove 3½" of soil over the interior portion of the slab, then slope the inner sides of the trench at 45° (see page 18). Set up temporary cross strings to check the depth as you work.

4. Add a 4" layer of compactible gravel over the entire excavation and rake it level. Compact the gravel thoroughly, using a rented plate compactor (see page 12).

Step B: Build the Form

1. Cut sheets of ¾" A-C plywood into six strips of equal width—about 7⅞", allowing for the saw cuts. To make sure the cuts are straight, use a table saw or a circular saw and straightedge.

2. Cut the plywood strips to length to create the sides of the form. Cut two sides 1½" long so they can overlap the remaining two sides. For sides that are longer than 8 ft., join two strips with a mending plate made of scrap plywood; fasten the plate to the back sides of the strips with 1¼" screws.

3. Assemble the form by fastening the corners together with screws. The form's inner dimensions must equal the outer dimensions of the slab.

A. *Measure down from the layout lines and temporary cross strings to check the depth of the excavation.*

B. *Assemble the form pieces with 2½" deck screws, then check the inner dimensions of the form. For long runs, join pieces with plywood mending plates.*

Step C: Set the Form

1. Cut 18"-long stakes from 2 × 3 lumber—you'll need one stake for every linear foot of form, plus one extra stake for each corner. Taper one end of each stake to a point.

2. Place the form in the trench and align it with the mason's lines. Drive a stake near the end of each side of the form, setting the stake edge against the form and driving down to 3" above grade.

3. Measuring down from the mason's lines, position the form 4" above grade. Tack the form to the stakes with partially driven 8d nails (driven through the form into the stakes). Measure the diagonals to make sure the form is square and check that the top of the form is level. Drive the nails completely.

4. Add a stake every 12" and drive them down below the top edge of the form. Secure the form with two 8d nails driven into each stake. As you work, check with a string line to make sure the form sides are straight and measure the diagonals to check for square.

Step D: Add the Metal Reinforcement

1. Lay out rows of 6 × 6" 10/10 welded wire mesh so their ends are 1" to 2" from the insides of the forms. Cut the mesh with bolt cutters or heavy pliers, and stand on the unrolled mesh as you cut, to prevent it from springing back. Overlap the rows of mesh by 6" and tie them together with tie wire.

2. Prop up the mesh with pieces of 1½"-thick brick pavers or metal bolsters.

3. Mark the layout of the J-bolts onto the top edges of the form, following your plan. (J-bolts typically are placed 4" to 6" from each corner and every 4 ft. in between.)

Step E: Pour the Slab

1. Starting at one end, fill in the form with concrete, using a shovel to distribute it. Use the shovel blade or a 2 × 4 to stab into the concrete to eliminate air pockets and settle it around the wire mesh and along the forms. Fill with concrete to the top of the form.

2. As the form fills, have two helpers screed the concrete, using a straight 2 × 4 or 2 × 6 that spans the form: Drag the screed board along the top of the form, working it back and forth in a sawing motion. Throw shovelfuls of concrete ahead of the screed board to fill low spots. The goal of screeding is to make the surface of the concrete perfectly flat and level, if not smooth.

3. Rap the outsides of the form with a hammer to settle the concrete along the inside faces of the form. This helps smooth the sides of the slab.

C. *Drive stakes every 12" to support the form, using the mason's lines to make sure the form remains straight.*

D. *Lay out rows of wire mesh, tie the rows together, then prop up the mesh with brick pavers or metal bolsters.*

Step F: Finish the Concrete & Set the J-bolts

1. Immediately after screeding the concrete, make one pass with a bull float to smooth the surface. Add small amounts of concrete to fill low spots created by the floating, then smooth those areas with the float. Floating forces the aggregate down and draws the water and sand to the surface.

2. Set the J-bolts into the concrete 1¾" from the outside edges of the slab. Work the bolts into the concrete by wiggling them slightly to eliminate air pockets. The bolts should be plumb and protrude 2½" from the slab surface. After setting each bolt, smooth the concrete around the bolt, using a magnesium or wood concrete float.

3. Watch the concrete carefully as it dries. The bull-floating will cause water (called *bleed water*) to rise, casting a sheen on the surface. Wait for the bleed water to disappear and the surface to become dull. Pressure-test the concrete for firmness by stepping on it with one foot: if your foot sinks ¼" or less, the concrete is ready to be finished. Note: Air-entrained concrete may have very little bleed water, so it's best to rely on the pressure test.

4. Float the concrete with a hand-held magnesium or wood float, working the float back and forth until the surface is smooth. If you can't reach

ESTIMATING CONCRETE

Calculate the amount of concrete needed for a slab of this design using this formula:

Width × Length × Depth, in ft. (of main slab)
Multiply by 1.5 (for footing edge and spillage)
Divide by 27 (to convert to cubic yards)

Example—for a 12 × 12-ft. slab:
12 × 12 × .29 (3½") = 41.76
41.76 × 1.5 = 62.64
62.64 ÷ 27 = 2.32 cubic yards

the entire slab from the sides, lay pieces of 2"-thick rigid foam insulation over the concrete and kneel on the insulation. Work backwards to cover up any impressions.

5. Use a concrete edging tool to round over the slab edge, running the edger between the slab and the form. If you want a very smooth finish, work the concrete with a trowel.

6. Let the concrete cure for 24 hours, then strip the forms. Wait an additional 24 hours before building on the slab.

E. *Screed the concrete after filling the form, using two people to screed, while a third fills low spots with a shovel.*

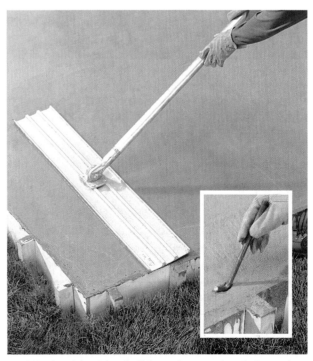

F. *Float the slab with a bull float, then set the J-bolts at the marked locations (inset).*

Framing

Framing is one of the most satisfying phases of a building project. Using basic tools and materials, you'll assemble the skeleton of the structure, piece-by-piece, and in the process learn the fundamentals of carpentry. The style of framing shown here is standard 2 × 4 framing, also called *stick framing*. For an alternative style, see the Timber-frame Garden Shed on pages 72 to 81.

The tools you'll use for most framing are the circular saw (and power miter saw, if you have one), framing square, level, chalk line, and, of course, a framing hammer. Nails used for most framing are called common nails. These have a larger diameter than box nails, making them stronger, but also more likely to split thinner stock. Box nails are better for siding, trim, and other non-structural materials. The three most commonly used nailing techniques are shown in the illustrations below. Some framing connections, such as where rafters meet wall plates, require metal anchors for increased strength.

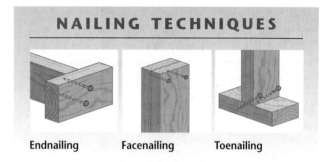

NAILING TECHNIQUES

Endnailing   Facenailing   Toenailing

Floor Framing

Floor frames for sheds are simple versions of house floor frames. They have outside, or *rim*, joists that are set on edge and nailed to the ends of the common joists. Gazebos have floor frames similar to decks, with angled joists that are connected to support beams with joist hangers (see sidebar, page 23). On top of floor frames, a layer of tongue-and-groove plywood (or decking boards, for a gazebo) provides the floor surface and adds strength to the frame. To prevent rot, always use pressure-treated lumber and galvanized nails and hardware for floor frames.

HOW TO BUILD A SHED FLOOR FRAME

Step A: Cut the Joists & Mark the Layout

1. Cut the two rim joists and the common joists to length, making sure both ends are square. Note that rim joists run the full length of the floor, while common joists are 3" shorter than the floor width.

2. Check the rim joists for crowning—arching along the narrow edges. Pick up one end of the board and hold it flat. With one eye closed, sight down the narrow edges. If the board arches, even slightly, mark the edge on the top (convex) side of the arch. This is the crowned edge and should always be installed facing up. If the board is crowned in both directions, mark the edge with the most significant crowning.

3. Lay one rim joist flat on top of the other so the edges and ends are flush and the crowned edges are on the same side. Tack the joists together with a few 8d nails. Turn the joists on-edge and mark the common joist layout on the top edges: Mark 1½" and 15¼" from the end of one joist. Then, measuring from the 15¼" mark, make a mark every 16"—at 32", 48", 64" and so on, to the end of the board (if the plan calls for 24" spacing, make a mark at 1½" and 23¼", then every 24" from there). Don't worry if the last space before the opposite end joist isn't as

---

TOOLS & MATERIALS

Circular saw	8d and 16d galv. common nails
Square	¾" tongue-and-groove exterior-grade plywood
Pressure-treated 2 × lumber	

A. *Tack together the rim joists, then mark the joist layout. Use a square to transfer the marks to the second rim joist.*

wide as the others. Make a mark 1½" in from the remaining end. After each mark, draw a small X designating to which side of the line the joist goes—this is a handy framers' trick to prevent confusion. This layout ensures that the edges of a 4-ft. or 8-ft. board or sheet will fall, or *break*, on the center of a joist.

4. Using a square, draw lines through each of the layout marks, carrying them over to the other rim joist. Draw Xs on the other joist, as well. Separate the joists and remove the nails.

Step B: Assemble & Square the Frame

1. Check the two end joists for crowning, then nail them between the rim joists so their outside faces are flush with the rim joist ends and the top edges are flush. Drive two 16d galvanized common nails through the rim joists and into the ends of the end joists, positioning the nails about ¾" from the top and bottom edges.

2. Install the remaining joists, making sure the crowned edges are facing up.

3. Check the frame for squareness by measuring diagonally from corner to corner: when the measurements are equal, the frame is square. To adjust the frame, apply inward pressure to the corners with the longer measurement.

4. If you're building the floor over skids, secure each joist to the outside skids with a metal anchor and toenail the joists to the internal skid(s) with 16d galvanized nails.

Step C: Install the Plywood Floor

1. Lay a full sheet of ¾" tongue-and-groove exterior-grade plywood over the frame so the groove side is flush with a rim joist and one end is flush with an end joist. Fasten the plywood to the joists with 8d galvanized nails driven every 6" along the edges and every 8" in the field of the sheet. Do not nail along the tongue edge until the next row of plywood is in place.

2. Cut the second piece to fit next to the first, allowing for a ⅛" gap between the sheets. Install the second sheet with its outside edges flush with the frame.

3. Start the next row with a full sheet (ripped to width, if necessary). Install the sheet starting from the corner opposite the first sheet, so the joints between rows are offset. Make sure the tongue-and-groove joint is tight; if necessary, use a wood block and a sledgehammer to close the joint.

4. Cut and install the remaining piece of plywood.

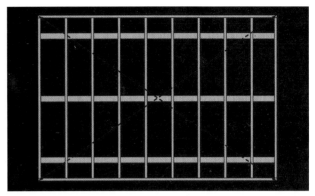

B. *Measure diagonally from corner to corner: If the measurements are equal, the frame is square.*

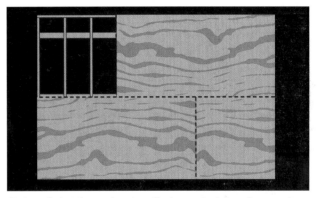

C. *Install the plywood perpendicular to the joists. Start each row with a full sheet and stagger the end-joints between rows.*

INSTALLING JOIST HANGERS

Mark the joist layout onto the header or beam and use a square to draw parallel lines that represent the outer edges of the joist. Position the hanger with one side flush to a joist outline, and fasten it with joist hanger nails (1½") or 10d or 16d galvanized common nails (**top**). Using a scrap piece of joist as a spacer, close the hanger around the spacer. Check the position of the spacer's top edge, then nail the free side of the hanger in place (**middle**). To install the joist, set it completely into the hanger and fasten it through the hanger holes with joist nails (**bottom**).

Wall Framing

Standard framed walls have vertical 2×4 *studs* nailed between horizontal top and bottom *plates*. The top plates are doubled to provide additional

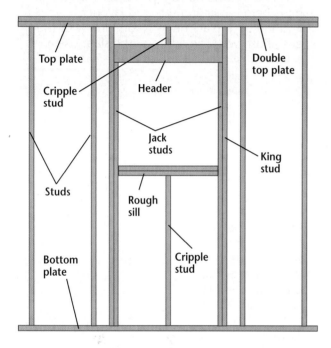

support for the roof frame and to strengthen the wall connections. Door and window frames are made up of *king* studs; a *header*, which supports *cripple* studs above the opening; and *jack* studs, which support the header. A window frame also has a *rough sill* and cripple studs below the opening. The opening defined by the frame is called the *rough opening*. Wall frames gain rigidity from plywood sheathing or siding.

Building walls involves three major phases: laying out and framing the walls; raising the walls; and tying the walls together and adding the double top plates. Note: If your building has a concrete slab floor, use pressure-treated lumber for the bottom plates and anchor the plates to the J-bolts set in the slab (see page 25).

TOOLS & MATERIALS

Broom	2 × lumber
Circular saw or power miter saw	8d, 10d, and 16d common nails
Square	½" plywood
4-ft. level	Construction adhesive
Handsaw	

HOW TO FRAME WALLS

Step A: Mark the Bottom-plate Layout Lines

1. Sweep off the floor and make sure it's dry. Cut a short (about 4" to 6") piece of plate material to use as a spacer. Position the spacer at one corner of the floor, with its outside edge flush with the outside of the floor frame. Mark a pencil line along the inside edge of the spacer.

2. Use the spacer to mark the wall ends at each corner of the floor (eight marks total). Snap chalk lines through the marks. These lines represent the inside edges of the bottom plates.

Step B: Lay Out the Plates

1. Measure along the plate layout lines to find the lengths of the plates. Note: Follow your project plans to determine which walls run to the edges of the building (called *through* walls) and which butt into the other walls (called *butt* walls).

2. Select straight lumber for the plates. Cut a top and bottom plate for the first wall, making sure their dimensions are the same. Use a circular saw or a power miter saw, but make sure both ends are square. Lay the bottom plate flat on the floor and set the top plate on top of it. Make sure their edges and ends are flush, then tack the plates together with a few 8d nails.

3. Turn the plates on-edge and mark the stud layout onto the front edges.

A. *Use a block cut from plate material to lay out the bottom plates. Mark at the ends of each wall then snap a chalk line.*

If the wall is a through wall, make a mark at 1½" and 2¾" to mark the end stud and extra corner stud. Then, mark at 15¼" (for 16" on-center spacing) or 23¼" (for 24" on-center spacing)—measuring from this mark, make a mark every 16" (or 24") to the end of the plates. Make a mark 1½" in from the opposite end. Following your plan, draw an X next to each mark, designating to which side of the line the stud goes.

Mark the king and jack studs with a K and J respectively, and mark the cripple studs with a C.

If the wall is a butt wall, mark the plate at 1½", then move the tape so the 3½" tape mark is aligned with the end of the plate. Keeping the tape at that position, mark at 15¼" (for 16" spacing) or 23¼" (for 24" spacing) then mark every 16" (or 24") from there. The 3½" that are "buried" account for the width of the through wall.

4. Using a square, draw lines through each of the layout marks, carrying them over to the other plate. Draw Xs on the other plate, as well.

Step C: Cut the Studs & Build the Headers

1. Cut the studs to length, following the framing plan; make sure both ends are square. (Before cutting, give each stud a quick inspection to check for excessive bowing or crowning; reserve any bad studs for scrap or blocking.)

2. Select straight lumber for the door-frame studs.

SECURING PLATES TO CONCRETE SLABS

When building walls over a concrete slab, drill holes in the bottom plates for the anchor bolts before marking the stud layouts. Position each plate on its layout line with the ends flush with the edges of the slab. Use a square to mark the edges of the bolt onto the plate (**top photo**). Measure from the layout line to the bolt center and transfer that dimension to the plate. Drill holes through the plates slightly larger in diameter than the bolts. After raising the walls, anchor the plates to the bolts with washers and nuts (**bottom photo**).

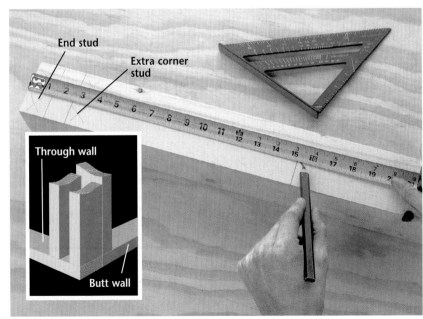

B. *Mark the stud layout onto the wall plates, designating the stud locations with Xs. Through walls have an extra corner stud 2¾" from each end.*

C. *Construct the headers from 2 × lumber and a ½" plywood spacer.*

Cut the jack studs to equal the height of the rough opening minus 1½" (this accounts for the thickness of the bottom plate); cut the jack studs for the window frame to equal the height of the top of the rough opening minus 1½". Cut the king studs the same length as the common studs.

3. To build the headers, cut two pieces of 2 × lumber (using the size prescribed by the plans) to equal the width of the rough opening plus 3". Check the boards for crowning, and mark the top edges (see Step A, page 22). Cut a piece of ½" plywood to the same dimensions as the lumber pieces.

4. Apply two wavy beads of construction adhesive to each side of the plywood and sandwich the lumber pieces around the plywood, keeping all edges flush. Nail the header together with pairs of 16d common nails spaced about 12" apart. Drive the nails at a slight angle so they won't protrude from the other side. Nail from both sides of the header.

Step D: Assemble the Wall

1. Separate the marked plates and remove the nails. Position the plates on-edge, about 8 ft. apart, with the marked edges facing up.

2. Set the studs on-edge between the plates, following the layout marks. Before setting the door- or window-frame studs, facenail the jack studs to the inside faces of the king studs with 10d common nails staggered and spaced every 12"; make sure the bottom ends and side edges are flush.

3. Nail all of the studs to the bottom plate, then to the top plate. Position each stud on its layout mark so its front edge is flush with the plate edge, and nail through the plate and into the stud end with two 16d common nails (use galvanized nails on the bottom plate if your floor is concrete). Drive the nails about ¾" in from the plate edges.

4. Set the header in place above the jack studs and nail through the king studs and into the header ends with 16d nails—use four nails on each end for a 2 × 6 header, and six for a 2 × 8 header.

For a window frame, measure up from the bottom of the bottom plate and mark the top of the sill on the inside faces of the jack studs—this defines the bottom of the rough opening. Cut two sill pieces to fit between the jack studs and nail them together with 10d nails. Toenail the sill to the jack studs with 16d nails.

5. Cut the cripple studs to fit between the header and the top plate (and the sill and bottom plate, for window frames). Toenail the cripple studs to the plates and headers (and sill) with two 8d nails on one side and one more through the center on the other side.

D. *Frame the walls with 16d nails endnailed through the plates into the studs. Toenail cripples to headers with 8d nails.*

E. *Install a diagonal brace to keep the wall square. Make sure the brace ends won't interfere with the construction.*

Step E: Square the Wall Frame

1. Check the wall frame for squareness by measuring diagonally from corner to corner: when the measurements are equal, the frame is square. To adjust the frame, apply inward pressure to the corners with the longer measurement.

2. When the frame is perfectly square, install a temporary 1 × 4 or 2 × 4 brace diagonally across the studs and plates. Nail the brace to the frame with 8d nails. Use two nails on the plates and on every other stud. To stabilize the structure, leave the wall braces in place until the walls are sheathed or sided.

3. At each end of the wall, attach a board to brace the wall upright after it is raised; nail it to the end stud with one 16d nail. Note: Install only one end brace for the second and third walls; no end brace is needed for the final wall.

Step F: Raise the Wall

1. With a helper, lift the top end of the wall and set the bottom plate on the layout lines you snapped in Step A. Swing out the free ends of the end braces and tack them to the floor frame to keep the wall upright. If you have a slab floor, nail the braces to stakes in the ground.

2. Fine-tune the wall position so the bottom plate is flush with the chalk line, then nail the plate to the floor with 16d nails. Drive a nail every 16" and stagger them so that half go into the rim joist and half go into the common joists. Do not nail the plate inside the door opening.

3. Pull the nails at the bottom ends of the end braces, and adjust the wall until it is perfectly plumb, using a 4-ft. level; set the level against a few different studs to get an accurate reading. Reattach the end braces with 16d nails.

Step G: Complete the Wall Frames & Install the Double Top Plates

1. Build and raise the remaining walls, following the same procedure used for the first wall. After each wall is plumbed and braced in position, nail together the end studs of the adjacent walls with 16d nails, driven every 12". Make sure the wall ends are flush.

2. Cut the double top plates from 2 × 4 lumber. The double top plates must overlap the top plate joints, so that on through walls, the double plate is 3½" shorter on each end than the top plate; on butt walls, the double plate is 3½" longer on each end. Nail the double top plates to the top plates with 10d nails. Drive two nails at the ends of the plates that overlap intersecting walls, and one nail every 16" in between.

3. Use a handsaw or reciprocating saw to cut out the bottom plate in the door opening.

F. *Nail the bottom plate to the floor frame, then plumb the wall and secure it with end braces.*

G. *Nail together the corner studs of intersecting walls (inset). Add the double top plates, overlapping the wall corners.*

Roof Framing

A roof frame is an important structure not only because it supports the roofing and helps keep the building dry, but because its style and shape have a great impact on the character of the building, the feel of the interior space, and the amount of storage space available.

There are four common roof types shown in this book. A *gable* roof is the classic, triangular design, with two sloped sides meeting at the peak, and flat ends (called *gable ends*). *Gambrel* roofs are like gable roofs with an extra joint on each side, resulting in two different slopes. A *hip* roof is structurally similar to a gable, but has no gable ends. *Shed* roofs are the simplest style, with only one sloped plane. They can be built with frames or, for small structures, a sheet of plywood.

All of these roof styles have a designated slope, which is the degree of angle of each side. The slope is expressed in a ratio that states the number of inches of vertical rise per 12" of horizontal run. For example, a roof that rises 6" for every 12" of run is said to have a slope of 6-in-12. Roof slope is indicated in plan drawings by a triangular symbol known as the *roof-slope indicator* (see page 29). You'll use the roof slope to lay out rafters and fascia.

In standard roof framing, rafters are the principal structural members, rising from the walls to the ridge board (or *hub*, in gazebos) at the peak of the roof. Rafters in outbuildings typically are made from 2 × 4s or 2 × 6s, are spaced 16" or 24" on center, and are installed perpendicular to the length of the building. To keep the roof planes from spreading apart, *rafter ties*, or *collar ties*, are nailed between opposing rafters to form a structural triangle. With shed-style roofs, the rafters span from wall-to-wall and no ridge board or ties are needed.

Ridge board — Roof sheathing — Collar tie — Rafters

The key to successful roof framing is making accurate cuts on the rafters. Take your time to cut the first two rafters, making any necessary adjustments, then use one as a pattern for marking the rest. The project on pages 29 through 31 shows you how to cut and install rafters in a gable roof frame, but the basic procedures are the same for gambrel and hip roofs.

As an alternative to rafter framing, you can take your plans to a truss manufacturer and have custom trusses built for your project. However, this will cost you more and probably will limit your storage space: the internal supports in truss frames leave little room for storage.

TOOLS & MATERIALS

Circular saw	2 × lumber
Framing square	8d, 10d, and 16d common nails
4-ft. level	

MARKING ANGLES WITH A SPEED SQUARE

A speed square is a handy tool for marking angled cuts—using the degree of the cut or the roof slope. Set the square flange against the board edge and align the PIVOT point with the top of the cut. Pivot the square until the board edge is aligned with the desired DEGREE marking or the rise of the roof slope, indicated in the row of COMMON numbers. Mark along the right-angle edge of the square.

Pivot point

Common markings

Degree markings

HOW TO BUILD A ROOF FRAME

Note: The following instructions are based on the sample rafter template shown here, which is designed for a 6-in-12 roof slope.

Step A: Mark the Plumb Cuts

1. Select a straight board to use for the pattern rafter. Mark the top plumb cut near one end of the board: Position a framing square with the 6" mark of the tongue (short part) and the 12" mark of the blade (wide part) on the top edge of the board. Draw a pencil line along the outside edge of the tongue.

2. Starting from the top of the plumb-cut mark, measure along the top edge of the board and mark the overall length of the rafter, then use the square to transfer this mark to the bottom edge of the board. Position the square so the tongue points down, and align the 6" mark of the tongue and the 12" mark of the blade with the bottom board edge, while aligning the tongue with the overall length mark. Draw a line along the tongue. If the bottom end cut of the rafter is square (perpendicular to the edges) rather than parallel to the top end, mark a square cut at the overall length mark.

Step B: Mark the Bird's Mouth Cuts

1. Measure from the bottom of the lower plumb cut and mark the plumb cut of the bird's mouth. Position the square as you did for the lower plumb cut and draw a line across the board face at the new mark.

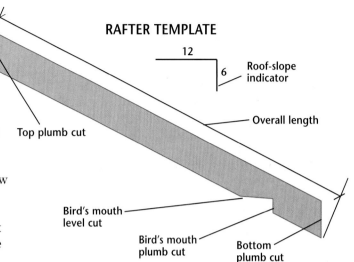

RAFTER TEMPLATE

12

6 — Roof-slope indicator

Overall length

Top plumb cut

Bird's mouth level cut

Bird's mouth plumb cut

Bottom plumb cut

2. Measure along the bird's mouth plumb cut and mark the bird's mouth level cut. Use the square to draw the level cut—it must be perpendicular to the bird's mouth plumb cut.

Step C: Make the Cuts

1. Cut the rafter ends at the plumb-cut lines, using a circular saw or power miter saw.

2. Set the base of a circular saw to cut at the maximum depth. Make the bird's mouth cuts, overcutting slightly to complete the cut through the thickness of the board. As an alternative to overcutting (for aesthetic reasons), you can stop the circular saw at the line intersections, then finish the cuts with a handsaw.

A. *Position the framing square at the 6" and 12" marks to draw the top and bottom plumb-cut lines.*

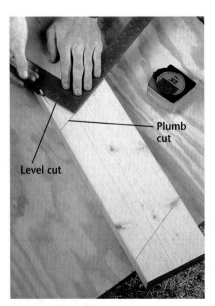

B. *Mark the bird's mouth level cut by squaring off of the bird's mouth plumb cut.*

C. *Cut the bird's mouth by overcutting the lines just until the blade cuts entirely through the board.*

D. *Test-fit the pattern rafters, using a spacer made of 2 × lumber to represent the ridge board.*

E. *Mark the rafter layout onto the wall plates and the ridge board, starting from the same end of the building for each.*

F. *Endnail the first rafter to the ridge, then toenail the second. Reinforce the bottom connection with a metal anchor (inset).*

3. Select another straight board to use as a second pattern rafter. Use the original pattern rafter to trace the cutting lines onto the duplicate, then make the cuts.

Step D: Test-fit the Rafters

1. Cut a 12"-long spacer block from 2 × 6 or 2 × 8 material.

2. With a helper or two, set the two rafters in place on top of the walls, holding the spacer block between the top rafter ends. Make sure the rafters are in line with each other (perpendicular to the walls) and are plumb.

3. Check the cuts for fit: the top-end plumb cuts should meet flush with the spacer block, and the bird's mouths should sit flush against the wall plates. Make sure the top ends are at the same elevation. Recut any angles that don't fit and test-fit the rafters again.

4. Write "PAT" on the pattern rafter, then use it to trace the cutting lines onto the remaining rafters. Before marking, check each rafter for crowning and mark the crowned edge (see Step A, on page 22); always install the crowned edge up. If your building has overhangs at the gable ends, mark the end cuts for the overhang rafters but not the bird's mouth cuts—overhang rafters don't have them. Also, if you have the fascia material on-hand, use the pattern rafter to mark the angle for the top ends of the fascia boards (see page 32).

5. Cut the remaining rafters.

Step E: Lay Out the Wall Plates & Ridge Board

Note: Start the rafter layouts from the ends of the walls where you started the wall stud layouts. This ensures the rafters will fall above the studs. Install rafters aligned with the end studs but not the extra corner studs.

1. Make a mark on the top wall plate 1½" in from the end. Then, mark at 15¼" (for 16" on-center spacing) or 23¼" (for 24" on-center spacing)—measuring from this mark, make a mark every 16" (or 24") to the end of the wall. Make a mark 1½" in from the remaining end. Following your plan, draw an X next to each mark, designating to which side of the line the rafter goes.

2. Mark the wall on the other side of the building, starting from the same end.

3. Cut the ridge board to length, using the plan dimensions. Check the board for crowning, then lay it on top of the walls next to one of the marked plates, making sure it overhangs the end walls equally at both ends. Use a square to transfer the

rafter layout onto both faces of the ridge board.

Step F: Install the Rafters

1. You'll need a couple of helpers and a long, straight 2×4 to get the rafters started. Lay the first two rafters on top of the wall, then nail the 2×4 to the far end of the ridge board to serve as a temporary support. Set up the rafters at the end of the walls and hold the free end of the ridge board in place between them. Have a helper tack the rafters to the wall plates. Hold a level on the ridge board and make sure it's level, then have a helper tack the support to the far wall to keep the ridge level.

2. Slide one rafter a few inches to the side and endnail the other rafter through the ridge board with three 16d common nails (use two nails for 2×4 rafters). Slide the other rafter onto its layout mark and toenail it to the ridge with four 16d nails (three for 2×4s). Toenail the lower end of each rafter to the wall plate with two 16d nails, then reinforce the joint with a metal anchor, using the nails specified by the manufacturer.

3. Make sure the rafters are plumb and the ridge is level. Install the remaining rafters, checking for plumb and level periodically as you work.

Step G: Install the Collar Ties

1. Cut the collar ties (or rafter ties) to span between opposing rafters at the prescribed elevation, angle-cutting the ends to match the roof slope.

2. Position the collar tie ends against the rafter faces so the ends are about ½" from the rafters edges. Make sure the ties are level, then facenail them to the rafters with three 10d common nails at each end.

Step H: Frame the Gable Wall

Note: Gable walls consist of top plates that attach to the undersides of the end rafters, and short studs set on top of the wall plates (see page 10). They appear only on gable and gambrel roofs.

1. Cut the top plates to extend from the side of the ridge board to the wall plates. Angle-cut the ends so they meet flush with the ridge and wall plate. The top-end angle matches the rafter plumb cut; the bottom angle matches the level cut of the bird's mouth.

2. Fasten the plates to the rafters so the front plate edges are flush with the outside faces of the rafters; use 16d nails.

3. Mark the gable stud layout onto the wall plate, then use a level to transfer the layout to the gable plates. Cut the gable studs to fit, angle-cutting the ends to match the roof slope. Install the gable studs with 8d toenails. Also install a square-cut stud directly under the ridge board.

Step I: Build the Gable Overhang (Gable & Gambrel Roofs)

Note: Gable overhangs are built with additional rafters installed at the gable ends (see page 10). They are supported by the ridge board and blocks—called *lookouts*—attached to the end rafters.

1. Mark the layouts for the lookouts onto the end rafters, following the project plan. Cut the lookouts and toenail them to the rafters with 8d nails (or endnail them with 16d nails) so that the top edges of the blocks are flush with, and parallel to, the tops of the rafters.

2. Install the overhang rafters over the ends of the lookouts with 16d endnails.

G. *Angle-cut the ends of the collar ties to match the roof slope and facenail the ties to the rafters*

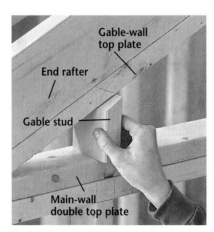

H. *Mark the gable stud layout onto the main-wall top plate and gable-wall top plate, then install the gable studs.*

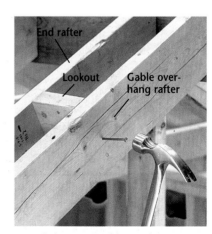

I. *Nail the outer gable overhang rafters to the lookouts, making sure the top edges of the rafters are flush.*

Roofing

The roofing phase typically follows the framing, for most building projects. As it's presented here, roofing includes installing the fascia board, the roof sheathing, and of course, the shingles or other material. You'll also see how to install roof vents.

Fascia board is 1 × trim material, typically made of cedar, that covers the ends of the rafters. On gable and gambrel roofs, fascia also covers the end (or gable overhang) rafters. Sheathing is the structural deck of the roof. Depending on the type of roofing used, the sheathing may be plywood, tongue-&-groove decking boards (see page 96), or spaced 1 × or 2 × lumber.

As for the roofing, deciding on a material is a matter of personal taste and practicality. Three common types used for outbuildings are covered here: asphalt shingles, cedar shingles, and metal roofing.

Asphalt shingles are the standard roofing material for outbuildings, just as they are for houses. For the money, asphalt shingles are the most durable and low-maintenance material available, and they come in a wide range of colors and styles.

Cedar shingles are a big step up in price from asphalt, but their visual appeal is undeniable. The type shown here is the factory-sawn shingle with flat, tapered sides. Cedar shingles are less expensive and easier to install than hand-split cedar shakes.

Metal roofing has been used for centuries on everything from chicken coops to cathedrals, and in recent years it has become increasingly popular in residential construction. Modern forms of metal roofing are extremely durable and easy to install, and they still make that nice sound when it rains.

Fascia & Sheathing

Fascia board and roof sheathing are always installed before the roofing, but which one you install first is up to you. Some buildings also have a 1 × or 2 × board installed behind the fascia, called *subfascia*. Made of rough lumber, the subfascia helps compensate for inconsistency in rafter length, ensuring the fascia will be straight. It also provides a continuous nailing surface for the fascia.

The type of sheathing you use depends on the roof covering. Use CDX plywood (it's exterior-grade) for asphalt and cedar shingles. Depending on the building design, the fascia may be installed flush with the top of the sheathing, or the plywood may overlap the fascia. If you install the fascia first, cut spacers from the sheathing stock and use them when measuring and installing the fascia. Both shingle types must be installed over a layer of 15# building paper (also called *tar paper* or *roofing felt*), which goes on after the sheathing and fascia. The paper protects the sheathing from moisture and prevents the shingles from bonding to it.

As an alternative to plywood sheathing, you can use decking boards as a shingle underlayment. Typically sold in ¾ dimension (1¹⁄₁₆" thick), board sheathing creates an attractive "ceiling" for the inside of a building, and the nails won't show through as they do with plywood sheathing.

For metal roofing, install *purlins*—evenly spaced, parallel rows of 1 × or 2 × boards nailed perpendicularly to the rafters. Install the fascia over the ends of the purlins, flush with the tops.

TOOLS & MATERIALS

Framing square	6d and 8d galvanized finish nails
Circular saw	CDX plywood roof sheathing
Stapler	8d box nails
Fascia & trim material	15# building paper

HOW TO INSTALL FASCIA BOARD

Note: This procedure includes the steps for installing fascia on a gable roof. The basic steps are the same for a gambrel roof. For a hip roof, which has no gable ends, skip Step A and start your installation by tacking the first fascia board to the rafter ends, then working from there.

To install subfascia, follow the same procedure used for fascia, but don't worry about mitering the ends—just overlap the boards at the corners.

Step A: Cut & Fit the Gable-end Fascia

1. Mark a plumb cut on the top end of the first fascia board: If you didn't mark the fascia boards with the pattern rafter (page 30), use a framing square to mark the plumb cut, following the same method used for marking rafters (see page 29). Make

the cut with a circular saw or power miter saw.

2. Hold the cut end of the fascia against the end rafter. If the fascia will be flush with the top of the sheathing, use spacers set on the rafter and position the top edge of the fascia flush with the spacers.

3. Have a helper mark the lower end for length by tracing along the rafter end onto the back side of the fascia. Make the cut with a 45° bevel. If you're using a circular saw, tilt the blade to 45° and follow the traced line; if you have a compound miter saw, rotate the blade to match the cutting line and tilt the blade to 45°.

4. Temporarily tack the fascia in place against the rafter with a couple of 8d galvanized finish nails. Repeat this process to mark, cut, and tack-up the opposing fascia piece, then do the same at the other gable end.

Step B: Install the Fascia Along the Eaves

1. Cut a 45° bevel on the end of another fascia piece and fit it against one of the pieces on the gable end. If the board is long enough to span the building, mark the opposite end to length. If you'll need two pieces to complete the eave, mark the board about ¼" from the far edge of a rafter; cut that end with a 45° bevel angled so the longer side of the board will be against the rafter. Cut the remaining piece with a 45° bevel angled in the opposite direction. This is known as a *scarf* joint—nail these with 8d galvanized finish nails and drill pilot holes to prevent splitting.

2. Make sure the corner joints fit well, then tack the fascia to the rafters.

3. Cut and tack-up the fascia along the other eave. Make sure all of the joints fit well, then fasten the fascia permanently with 8d galvanized finish nails: drive three nails into each rafter end and a pair of nails every 16" along the gable ends.

4. Lock-nail each corner joint with three 6d galvanized finish nails. If necessary, drill pilot holes to prevent splitting.

5. Install any additional trim, such as 1 × 2, called for by the plan. Miter the ends for best appearance.

A. *Mark the bottom end of the gable fascia by tracing along the end of the rafter (or the subfascia). If the fascia will be installed flush with the sheathing, use a spacer for positioning.*

B. *Fasten the fascia to the rafters (or subfascia) with 8d finish nails, then lock-nail the corner joints with 6d nails. Use scarf joints to join boards in long runs (inset).*

HOW TO INSTALL PLYWOOD SHEATHING & BUILDING PAPER

Step A: Install the Sheathing

1. Lay a full sheet of CDX plywood on top of the rafters at one of the lower corners of the roof. Position the edges of the sheet ⅛" from the fascia (or the outside edges of the rafters) and make sure the inside end of the sheet falls over the center of a rafter; trim the sheet, if necessary.

2. Fasten the sheet to the rafters with 8d box nails spaced every 6" along the edges and every 12" in the field of the sheet.

3. Cut and install the next sheet to complete the first row, leaving a ⅛" gap between the sheet ends.

4. Start the second row with a half-length sheet so the vertical joints will be staggered between rows. Measure from the top of the first row to the center of the ridge board, and rip the sheet to that dimension.

5. Install the first sheet of the second row, then cut and install the remaining sheet to complete the row.

6. Sheath the opposite side of the roof following the same process.

Step B: Install the Building Paper

Note: If you are installing asphalt shingles, add drip edge along the eaves before laying the building paper (see page 35).

1. Roll out 15# building paper across the roof along the eave edge. If you've installed drip edge, hold the paper flush with the drip edge; if there's no drip edge, overhang the fascia on the eave by ⅜". Overhang the gable ends by 1" to 2". (On hip roofs, overhang the hip ridges by 6".)

2. Secure the paper with staples driven about every 12".

3. Apply the remaining rows, each overlapping the preceding row by at least 2". Overhang the ridge by 6". Overlap any vertical joints by at least 4".

4. Install the paper on the other roof side(s), again overlapping the ridge by 6".

5. Trim the paper flush with the fascia on the gable ends.

A. *Install the plywood sheathing so the vertical joints are staggered between rows.*

B. *Apply building paper from the bottom up, so the lower paper is overlapped by the paper above it.*

Asphalt Shingles

Asphalt shingles come in a variety of styles, but most are based on the standard three-tab system, in which each shingle strip has notches creating three equally sized tabs on the lower half of the strip. When installed, the tabs cover the solid portion of the shingle below it, giving the appearance of individual shingles.

For durability, use fiberglass-based shingles rather than organic-based. Also check the packaging to make sure the shingles comply with the ASTM D 3462 standard for durability. If you choose a specialty style, such as a decorative shingle or a type that is made to appear natural (similar to wood or slate), check with the manufacturer for specific installation instructions.

Prepare the roof for shingles by installing building paper and metal drip edge along the roof perimeter. Drip edge covers the edges of the fascia and supports the shingle edges.

TOOLS & MATERIALS

Metal snips	Metal drip edge
Chalk line	Asphalt shingles
Utility knife	2d roofing nails
Straightedge	Roofing cement

HOW TO INSTALL ASPHALT SHINGLES
Step A: Install the Drip Edge

Note: Install drip edge along the eaves before applying building paper; install drip edge along the gable ends on top of the paper.

1. Cut a 45° miter on the end of a piece of drip edge, using metal snips. Hold the end flush with the corner of the fascia, and fasten the flange of the drip edge to the sheathing with roofing nails driven every 12". To prevent corrosion, use galvanized nails with galvanized drip edge and aluminum nails with aluminum edge. Overlap vertical joints by 2".

2. Apply the building paper over the entire roof (see page 34). Install drip edge along the gable ends, over the paper, cutting 45° miters to meet the ends of the eave drip edge. Overlap horizontal joints by 2", overlapping the higher piece on top of the lower. At the roof peak, trim the front flanges so the opposing edge pieces meet at a vertical joint.

Step B: Install the Starter Course of Shingles

1. Snap a chalk line 11½" up from the front edge of the drip edge (this will result in a ½" overlap for standard 12" shingles).

2. Trim off one-half (6") of the end tab of a shingle, using a utility knife and straightedge.

3. Position the shingle upside-down, so the tabs are on the chalk line and the half-tab overhangs the gable drip edge by ⅜". Fasten the shingle with four

A. *Install drip edge along the eaves over the sheathing. Add the building paper, then install edging along the gable ends.*

B. *Trim 6" from the end tab to begin the starter row. Position the starter course shingles upside down so the tabs point up.*

2d roofing nails, about 3½" up from the bottom edge: drive one below each tab, one 2" in from the gable edge, and one 1" from the inside edge. Drive the nails straight and set the heads just flush to avoid tearing the shingle.

4. Use full shingles for the remainder of the course, placing them upside down and butting their edges together. Trim the last shingle so it overhangs the gable edge by ⅜".

Step C: Install the Remaining Courses

1. Install the first course of shingles, starting with a full shingle. Position the tabs down and align the shingle edges with those in the starter course. Drive four nails into each shingle: one ⅝" above each tab, and one 1" in from each end, at the same level. Trim the last shingle to match the starter course.

2. Snap a chalk line on the building paper, 17" up from the bottom edge of the first course; this will result in a 5" exposure for each course.

3. Begin the second course with a full shingle, but overhang the end of the first course by ½ of a tab. Begin the third course by overhanging a full tab, then 1½ tabs for the fourth course. Start the fifth course with a full shingle aligned with the first course, to repeat the staggered pattern. Snap a chalk line for each course, maintaining a 5" exposure. After every few courses, measure from the ridge to the shingle edges to make sure the shingles are running parallel to the ridge. If necessary, make slight adjustments with each course until the

shingles are parallel to the ridge.

4. Trim the top course of shingles at the ridge. If you are working on a hip roof (gazebo), trim the shingles at each hip ridge.

5. Repeat the procedure to shingle the remaining side(s) of the roof. Overlap the ridge with the top course of shingles and nail them to the other roof side; do not overlap more than 5". On a hip roof, trim the shingles along the hip ridge.

Step D: Install the Ridge Caps

1. Cut ridge caps from standard shingle tabs: taper each tab along the side edges, starting from the top of the slots and cutting up to the top edge. Cut three caps from each shingle—you'll need one cap for every 5" of ridge.

2. Snap a chalk line across the shingles, 6" from the ridge. Starting at the gable ends (for a gable roof) or the bottom edge (for a hip roof), install the caps by bending them over the ridge and aligning one side edge with the chalk line. Fasten each cap with one nail on each roof side, 5½" from the finished (exposed) edge and 1" from the side edge. Maintain a 5" exposure for each shingle. Fasten the last shingle with a nail at each corner, then cover the nail heads with roofing cement.

3. Trim the overhanging shingles along the gable ends: Snap chalk lines along the gable ends, ⅜" from the drip edges (these should line up with the first, fifth, etc., courses). Trim the shingles at the lines. Cover any exposed nails with roofing cement.

C. *Stagger each course of shingles by ½ tab, repeating the pattern after overhanging the edge by 1½ tabs.*

D. *Divide the shingles into thirds, then trim the corners to create the shingle caps (inset). Install the caps at the ridge.*

INSTALLING ROOF VENTS

Roof vents, used in conjunction with soffit vents (page 44), can help keep the air in your shed cooler and cleaner. Vents are rated by square inches of ventilation area; most sheds need only two 68" roof vents and two to four 50" soffit vents.

Install roof vents centered between two rafters, about 16" to 24" from the ridge board. Cut a hole through the roof sheathing, following the manufacturer's instructions **(photo, right)**.

After applying building paper (page 34), center the vent over the hole, and trace around its base flange.

Install shingles to a point at least 2" inside the bottom of the outline—don't cover the hole.

Apply roofing cement to the underside of the base flange, then install the vent over the shingles, using rubber-gasket

roofing nails driven into all of the flange sides.

Shingle over the side and top vent flanges, leaving the bottom flange exposed; do not nail through the flanges with the shingle nails **(photo, below)**.

Cedar Shingles

Cedar shingles come in 16", 18", and 24" lengths and in random widths, generally between 3" and 10" wide. The exposure of the shingles depends on the slope of the roof and the length and quality of the shingles (check with the manufacturer). Because they're sold in a few different grades, make sure the shingles you get are good enough to be used as roofing. Also, be aware that galvanized nails may cause some staining or streaking on the shingles; if you can't accept that, use aluminum or stainless-steel nails.

The project shown here includes 18" shingles with a 5½" exposure installed on a gable roof. At the ridge, the shingles are covered with a 1 × cedar ridge cap, which is easier to install than cap shingles. If you want to shingle a hip roof (gazebo), consult a professional.

HOW TO INSTALL CEDAR SHINGLE ROOFING
Step A: Install the Starter Course

1. Apply building paper to the entire roof, overhanging the eaves by ⅜" (see page 34).

2. Position the first shingle in the starter course so it overhangs the gable edge by 1" and the eave edge by 1½". Tack or clamp a 2 × 4 spacer to the fascia to help set the overhang. Make sure the butt

TOOLS & MATERIALS

Utility knife	2 × 4 lumber
Chalk line	3d & 6d roofing nails
Circular saw	6d galvanized nails
Table saw	1 × 4 and 1 × 6 cedar
T-bevel	Caulk
Cedar shingles	

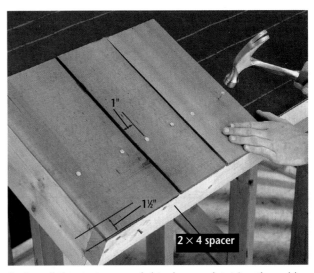

A. *Install the starter row of shingles, overhanging the gable end by ⅜" and the eave by 1½".*

(thick) end of the shingle is pointing down. Fasten the shingle with two 3d roofing nails, driven 4" up from the butt end and at least 1" from the side edges. Drive the nails just flush with the surface—countersinking creates a cavity that collects water.

3. Install the remaining shingles in the starter course, maintaining a ¼" to ⅜" gap between shingles. If necessary, trim the last shingle to width.

Step B: Install the Remaining Courses

1. Set the first shingle in the first course so its butt and outside edges are flush with the shingles in the starter course and it overlaps the shingle gap below by 1½". Fasten the shingle 1" to 2" above the exposure line and 1" from the side edges.

2. Install the remaining shingles in the first course, maintaining a ¼" to ⅜" gap between shingles.

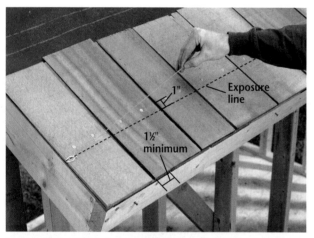

B. *Install the first course of shingles on top of the starter course, offsetting the shingle gaps 1½" between the courses.*

C. *Cover the ridge with 24" of building paper, then a course of trimmed shingles. Repeat with 12" of paper and shingles.*

3. Snap a chalk line across the shingles at the exposure line (5½" in this example). Install the second course, aligning the butt ends with the chalk line. Make sure shingle gaps are offset with the gaps in the first course by 1½".

4. Install the remaining courses, using chalk lines to set the exposure. Measure from the ridge periodically to make sure the courses are parallel to the ridge. Offset the shingle gaps by 1½" with the gaps in the preceding three courses—that is, any gaps that are aligned must be four courses apart. Add courses until the top (thin) ends of the shingles are within a few inches of the ridge.

5. Shingle the opposite side of the roof.

Step C: Shingle the Ridge

1. Cut a strip of building paper to 24" wide and as long as the ridge. Fold the paper in half and lay it over the ridge so it overlaps the shingles on both sides of the roof; tack it in place with staples.

2. Install another course of shingles on each side, trimming the top edges so they are flush with the ridge. Cut another strip of building paper 12" wide, fold it, and lay it over these shingles.

3. Install the final course on each side, trimming the ends flush with the ridge. Nail the shingles about 2½" from the ridge.

Step D: Install the Ridge Cap

1. Find the angle of the ridge using a T-bevel and two scraps of 1 × board: position the boards along the ridge with their edges butted together. Set the T-bevel to match the angle.

2. Transfer the angle to a table saw or circular saw and rip test pieces of 1 ×. Test-fit the pieces on the ridge, and adjust the angles as needed.

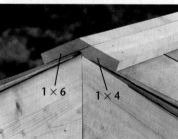

D. *Use a T-bevel and scrap boards to find the ridge angles, then cut the 1 × 4 and 1 × 6 for the ridge cap.*

3. Cut the 1 × 6 and 1 × 4 cap boards to run the length of the ridge. Join the boards with caulk and 6d galvanized box nails. Attach the cap to the ridge with 6d roofing nails driven every 12".

Metal Roofing

Metal roofing panels typically are available in 3-ft.-wide panels, with most styles using some form of standing seam design, which adds strength and provides means for joining sheets. You can buy the roofing through metal roofing suppliers and at home centers, but the former typically offer more color options, and they'll custom-cut the panels to fit your project. Most manufacturers supply rubber-washered nails or screws for a watertight seal—use the recommended fasteners to prevent premature rusting due to galvanic action (caused by contact between dissimilar metals).

Install metal roofing over 1×4 or 2×4 purlins nailed perpendicularly to the rafters at 12" to 24" on center—check with the manufacturer for purlin spacing and load requirements. At gable ends, add blocking between the purlins to provide a nailing surface for the end panels and drip edge.

HOW TO INSTALL METAL ROOFING

Step A: Install the Purlins

1. Mark the purlin layout on the top edges of the the rafters, and snap a chalk line for each row. Fasten 2×4 purlins to the rafters with 16d common nails; use 8d nails for 1×4s. Make sure the uppermost purlins will support the roofing ridge cap.

2. On the gable ends, cut blocking to fit between

TOOLS & MATERIALS

Chalk line	16d common nails
Circular saw	Metal roofing panels and pre-
Drill	formed ridge cap, with
1×4 or 2×4 lumber	fasteners

the purlins, and install it so the outside edges are flush with the outer faces of the outer rafters.

Step B: Install the Roof Panels

1. Set the first roof panel across the purlins so the finished side edge overhangs the gable-end fascia by 2" and the bottom end overhangs the eave by 2". Fasten the panel with self-tapping screws or roofing nails with rubber washers, following the manufacturer's directions for spacing.

2. Install the subsequent panels, overlapping each panel according to the manufacturer's directions.

3. Rotate the final panel 180° from the others, so the finished side edge is at the gable end. Overlap the preceding panel by as much as necessary so the finished edge overhangs the gable edge by 2". Fasten the final panel.

Step C: Install the Ridge Cap

1. Center the pre-formed ridge cap over the peak so it overlaps the roofing panels. Make sure the cap overhangs the gable ends equally on both sides. Note: some products include ridge-cap sealing strips.

2. Fasten the ridge cap to the top purlins.

A. *Install the purlins across the rafters, then add blocking at the gable ends.*

B. *Install the panels to the purlins using the manufacturer's fasteners.*

C. *Add the ridge cap at the roof peak, covering the panels on both roof sides.*

Siding & Trim

The siding and exterior trim not only provide an attractive skin for your building, they protect the structure from the weather. It's important to keep this function in mind as you install them: watch for areas where water can pool or trickle in, and make sure all unfinished edges and seams are covered or sealed with caulk.

Many siding manufacturers recommend staining or priming the back side of the siding (called *back-priming*) before installing it, which can help prevent the material from cupping or warping. Since conditions vary by region, ask your supplier about the best treatment for your siding, or contact the manufacturer.

The nails you use are another important consider-ation. All nails used outdoors must be corrosion-resistant, such as galvanized, aluminum, or stainless steel nails. Galvanized are the cheapest but can cause staining on unpainted (stained) cedar; aluminum nails won't stain, but can be difficult to drive; stain-less steel nails are expensive but are strong and are guaranteed not to stain or corrode. Ring- or spiral-shank siding nails offer the greatest holding power.

Apply a protective finish—stain, paint, or var-nish—to your siding and trim as soon as possible after installing them. Man-made products, although often factory-primed, are especially susceptible to water damage where hammer blows, nail holes, and cuts have marred the protective finish.

Horizontal Siding

Common types of horizontal siding include clap-board (also called *bevel* or *lap*), which is installed to overlap the piece below it, and Dolly Varden, shiplap, and drop styles, which have grooved lower edges that receive the top edge of the board beneath. All types come in a variety of solid woods, and lap siding is also available in faux-textured hard-board—an inexpensive alternative to solid wood.

Install horizontal siding over plywood wall sheath-ing and 15# building paper. For most applications, it's easiest to install the exterior trim (see page 44) first then install the siding to fit between the trim boards. This means that the doors and windows will be in place, too.

The siding shown in this project is a hardboard lap siding installed with a 6" exposure. The boards have been primed on both sides, which protects the back side from moisture and saves time when paint-ing the front side. Whichever siding you choose, check with the manufacturer regarding back-priming and moisture protection. Determine the overlap before starting. You can follow the manu-facturer's minimum (typically 1"), or use more over-lap so that the siding joints fall evenly at openings or along the tops of the walls.

HOW TO INSTALL HORIZONTAL SIDING
Step A: Install the Sheathing & Building Paper

1. Install ½" plywood sheathing (⅜" min. for 16" o.-c.; ½" for 24" o.-c.), starting at one corner of the building. Hold the side edge flush with the corner framing and the bottom edge flush with the bottom

TOOLS & MATERIALS

Circular saw	½" CDX plywood
Jig saw	6d box nails
Stapler	15# building paper
Utility knife	Siding
Chalk line	8d siding nails
Level	Caulk

A. *Install plywood sheathing over the entire frame, then sta-ple building paper over the sheathing.*

of the floor frame. Make sure the other side edge breaks on the center of a wall stud. The top edge should cover at least one of the wall plates. Nail the sheathing with 6d box nails, driven every 6" along the edges and 12" in the field of the sheet.

2. Install the remaining sheets, leaving a ⅛" gap between sheets. Overlap the sheathing at the corners. Sheath over window and door openings, then cut out the openings with a jig saw or reciprocating saw.

3. Apply 15# building paper in horizontal strips over the entire wall surface, using staples driven about every 12". Overlap horizontal joints by 2", vertical joints by 6", and corners by 12". Hold or trim the paper flush with the bottom of the floor frame. Wrap door and window openings with paper.

4. Install all exterior trim (see page 44), holding the corner and door trim ¾" below the floor framing. Install flashing over exposed doors and windows.

Step B: Install the Starter Strip & First Course

1. Cut 1"-wide starter strips of siding so there's enough to run the length of all of the walls. If the siding is beveled, cut only from the top edge of each piece, or use strips of plywood that match the thickness of the siding's top edge.

2. Position the starter strip along the bottom edge of the sheathing and fasten it to the framing with 8d siding nails.

3. Snap a chalk line above the bottom edge of the sheathing at a height equal to the width of the siding minus ¾". Mark the centers of the wall studs onto the building paper to facilitate nailing.

4. Cut the first course of siding to fit between the trim boards; make it snug but not so tight that you have to force the siding into place. Fasten the siding with one 8d siding nail driven at each stud location, about 1¼" from the bottom edge. If you need two boards to span the wall, center the inside ends over a stud, leaving a ⅛" gap between them; drive two nails at each end.

Step C: Install the Remaining Courses

1. Using the exposure dimension, measure from the top edge of the first course and snap a chalk line. Make sure the line is level; if it's not level, make slight adjustments over the next few courses.

2. Install the next course, aligning the top edge with the chalk line. Nail the siding just above the top edge of the course below, driving one nail at each stud. If the course has two boards, make sure the joint falls one or two studs away from the joint in the first course (stagger the joints for two more courses, then repeat the pattern at the original stud).

3. Snap chalk lines for the remaining courses, using the reveal dimension, and check the lines for level. Install the remaining courses. Mark angled cuts using a pattern made from scrap siding.

4. After completing one wall, use a level to transfer the siding layout onto the adjacent wall, so that the courses are aligned horizontally.

5. When all of the siding is installed, caulk all joints where siding meets trim or other pieces of siding.

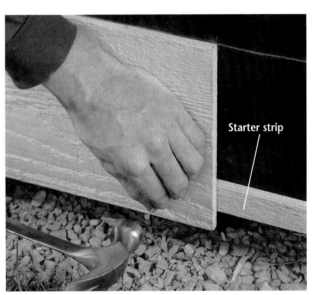

B. *Nail a starter strip along the edge of the sheathing, then snap a chalk line and install the first row of siding.*

C. *Drive siding nails into the studs, just above the preceding course (inset). Caulk all end-joints after the installation.*

Plywood Siding

Plywood siding is the least expensive and easiest to install of all the standard exterior finishes. It's available in 4 × 8-ft., 9-ft., and 10-ft. sheets; ⅜", ½", or ⅝" thicknesses; and in several styles, including striated, rough sawn, channel groove, and board-&-batten. The most common style, Texture 1-11 (shown here), is made to resemble vertical board siding and typically has ship-lap edges that form weather-proof vertical seams.

Another advantage of plywood siding is that the panels serve as bracing for framed walls, eliminating the need for sheathing. Plywood siding is exterior-grade, but the layered edges must be protected from moisture. For types with unmilled (square) edges, caulk the gap at vertical seams or install a 1 × 2 batten strip over the joint. All horizontal joints must have metal Z-flashing for moisture protection.

HOW TO INSTALL PLYWOOD SIDING
Step A: Install the First Row of Siding
1. Snap a chalk line for the top edges of the siding, accounting for the overhang at the bottom edge: for wood floors, overhang the bottom of the floor frame by ¾" to 1"; for slabs, overhang the top of the slab by 1".

2. Position the first sheet—vertically—at a corner so one side edge is flush with the corner framing and the other breaks on the center of a stud; hold the top edge on the chalk line. Check with a level to make sure the sheet is plumb, then fasten it with 8d galvanized finish nails, driven every 6" along the perimeter and every 12" in the field of the sheet.

3. Install the remaining sheets, checking each one for plumb and leaving a ⅛" gap between sheets. (For ship-lap edges, first fit the sheets tight, then draw a pencil line along the upper sheet's edge. Slide over the upper sheet ⅛", using the mark as a gauge.) At the joints, do not nail through both sheets with one nail. Overlap the sheets at the corners, if desired (they will be covered by trim, in any case). Apply siding over door and window openings, but do not nail into the headers if you will install flashing (see page 47). If you start with a trimmed sheet, place the cut edge at the corner.

Step B: Install the Flashing & Second Row
1. Install Z-flashing along the top edge of siding, using 6d galvanized box nails.

2. Install the upper row of siding, leaving a ⅛" gap above the flashing.

3. Cut out the door and window openings with a circular saw, jig saw, or reciprocating saw.

4. Install trim over the flashed joints and at the building corners (see page 44).

TOOLS & MATERIALS

Chalk line	8d galvanized finish nails
Level	6d galvanized box nails
Circular saw	Galvanized Z-flashing
Plywood siding	

A. *Install the plywood siding vertically. Plumb each sheet and fasten it to the framing with 6d nails.*

B. *Add galvanized metal flashing between rows of siding to prevent water from entering the seam.*

Tongue-&-Groove Vertical Siding

Solid-wood, tongue-and-groove board siding has an attractive, natural look that is well-suited for outdoor buildings. Standard sizes of siding are 1×4, 1×6, and 1×8, available in cedar, redwood, pine and other wood species. The type shown in this project is cedar 1×8 siding with V-grooves. Buy your siding long enough to run the full height of the building, because horizontal joints are difficult to make and they don't always look good.

Siding that is 6" wide (nominal dimension) or narrower can be *blindnailed* with angled nails driven at the base of the tongue only, so the heads are hidden by the groove of the next piece **(photo, right top)**; 8" or wider siding should be facenailed with two nails at each support **(photo, right bottom)**.

If your building is stick-framed, add 2×4 blocking between the studs at 24" on center to support the siding.

HOW TO INSTALL VERTICAL T-&-G SIDING

Step A: Add Blocking (if needed)

1. Snap horizontal chalk lines across the studs, 24" apart, measuring from the floor.

2. Cut 2×4 blocks to fit between the studs. Endnail the blocks to the studs with 16d nails. Position alternate blocks below the chalk line to facilitate nailing.

Step B: Install the Siding

1. If you are blindnailing the siding, position the first piece with the grooved edge flush with the corner framing; if you're facenailing, use either edge. Overhang the bottom of the board ¾" to 1" below the bottom of the floor framing (for wood floors) or 1" below the top of the slab (for concrete floors).

2. Hold a level along the leading edge to make sure the board is plumb, then fasten the board along the outside edge, every 16". For blindnailing, drive a 6d galvanized finish nail into each support—along the tongue; for facenailing, drive two 8d siding nails at each support, 1½" to 2" from the side edges.

3. Install the next board, fitting together the tongue-and-groove

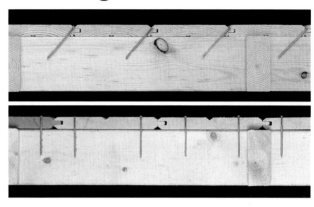

TOOLS & MATERIALS

Circular saw	2×4 blocking
Chalk line	16d nails
Level	Siding
	8d siding nails or 6d galvanized

joint. Nail at each support.

4. Install the remaining boards. Check every third or fourth board with the level to make sure it's plumb. Notch boards to fit flush around window and door openings; do not nail into the headers if you will install flashing (see page 47). To start a wall with a trimmed board, place the cut edge at the corner.

A. *Snap chalk lines at 24" intervals to guide the blocking placement. Endnail the blocking between the studs.*

B. *Plumb every third or fourth board with a level, making minor adjustments to the joints, if necessary.*

FINISHING ROOF OVERHANGS

A common method for finishing the underside of a roof overhang is to install soffit panels that enclose the rafter ends. Soffits can be attached directly to the rafters or to horizontal blocking that extends back to the wall. An alternative to soffitting is leaving the rafter ends exposed. With this application, the wall siding is notched to fit around the rafters.

A roof overhang should also include means for ventilating the building. With soffits, this can be achieved with soffit vents—metal grates (available in rectangular, plug, and strip styles) that cover holes cut into the soffit panels. Exposed overhangs are by nature ventilated but should have bug screen to seal the gaps between the walls and the roof sheathing. To increase ventilation, you can also install roof vents (see page 37).

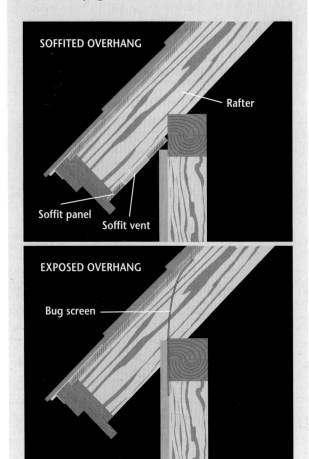

SOFFITED OVERHANG

Rafter

Soffit panel

Soffit vent

EXPOSED OVERHANG

Bug screen

Trim

Trim includes the boards that conceal building seams, cover gaps around window and door frames, finish corners, and perform other decorative and weatherproofing functions. For sheds and

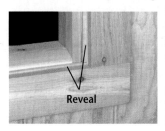

Reveal

Window trim with butt joints

Window trim with miter joints

outbuildings, simple trim details with 1×3, 1×4, or 1×6 cedar boards work well.

The type of siding you use will determine when to install the trim. For horizontal siding, install the trim first; for most other types, install the trim over the siding. If the trim is installed before the siding, make sure it's level and plumb —otherwise, you'll have to cut custom angles on the siding ends.

The simplest method for installing trim is to use butt joints. A slightly fancier alternative is to miter them. Trim joints are most noticeable on window and door trim **(see photos, above)**, but you can miter corner trim, too.

To install window and door trim with butt joints, add the head trim first, then cut the two side pieces to fit. Install mitered trim pieces on opposing sides, (that is, top-bottom, then sides, or vice versa). Leave a ¼" reveal for all window and door trim. This adds interest and makes bowed jambs less noticeable. Exposed doors and windows must have flashing above the trim (see page 47).

To install corner trim, cut two pieces to length, then nail them together at a right angle, using 6d or 8d galvanized box nails or finish nails. Set the trim on the corner, plumb it with a level, and nail it to the framing with 8d galvanized box or finish nails.

Nail corner trim pieces together before installing them.

Doors & Windows

Shed doors and windows can be either prehung (factory-built) or homemade. The shed projects in this book include plans for making your own doors and windows. They're simple designs using basic materials and can be built in an hour or two.

To keep water out, install flashing above the trim of any doors or windows that are exposed—that is, without a roof overhang above. If security is a concern, install a deadbolt for a pre-hung door or a hasp latch and padlock for a homemade door.

Prehung Doors & Windows

Prehung door and window units come in standard sizes, or they can be ordered in custom sizes, though at a higher price. Before framing the walls of your shed, select a door or window and confirm its exact dimensions before sizing the rough openings; be sure to use the outer dimensions of the unit's frame, not of the door or window itself.

Most exterior doors have preattached trim, called *brick molding*, on the outsides of the jambs. You can remove this if you want to add your own trim.

TOOLS & MATERIALS

Level	16d galvanized casing nails
Handsaw	(door) or 1¾" roofing nails
Nail set	(window)
Door or window unit	
Tapered cedar shims	

HOW TO INSTALL A PREHUNG WINDOW

Note: Window installations vary by product and manufacturer; follow the specific instructions provided for your window, including the steps for preparing the rough opening, shimming, flashing, etc. Shown here are the basic steps for installing a utility window with a nailing flange.

Step A: Set & Shim the Window

1. Set the window into the rough opening and center it between the sides. Place pairs of tapered shims directly beneath the side jambs and at the center of the sill; position the shims so the tapered ends are opposed to form a flat surface.

2. From outside, drive one 1¾" roofing nail through the nailing flange at one of the lower corners of the window, but do not drive the nail completely (see Step B).

Step B: Level & Fasten the Window

1. Place a level across the sill or top of the jamb,

A. *Add pairs of tapered shims under the side window jambs and under the center of the sill.*

B. *Level the window, then fasten the unit in place with roofing nails driven through the nailing flange.*

and adjust the shims until the window is perfectly level.

2. Drive one nail through the nailing flange at each corner of the window. Check the window operation to make sure it's smooth, then complete the nailing, following the manufacturer's instructions for spacing.

3. If the manufacturer recommends leaving the shims in place, trim the shims with a utility knife, then glue them in place with construction adhesive.

HOW TO INSTALL A PREHUNG DOOR
Step A: Plumb & Fasten the Hinge Jamb

1. Cut out the bottom plate inside the rough opening, using a handsaw. Remove any bracing or nails installed to protect the door during shipping.

2. Set the door into the opening and center it between the sides. Push the brick molding flat against the sheathing or siding; if there's no molding, position the outside edge of the jamb flush with the siding or sheathing. Insert pairs of tapered shims (with the tapered ends opposed to form a flat surface) between the hinge jamb and the framing. Add shims at the top and bottom and at each hinge location.

3. Starting with the top shims, check the hinge jamb with a level to make sure it's plumb, and adjust the shims as needed. Nail through the jamb and shims and into the framing with one 16d casing nail. Repeat at the remaining shim locations.

Step B: Secure the Latch & Head Jambs

1. Standing inside the shed, close the door, and examine the gap between the door and latch jamb. Starting at the top of the latch jamb, install shims between the jamb and the framing. Check the gap to make sure you're not bowing the jamb. Fasten the jamb and shims with one 16d casing nail.

2. Shim and fasten the latch jamb at four more locations, level with the hinge-side shims, making sure the gap along the door remains consistent.

3. Shim and fasten the head jamb at two locations. For added support, you can replace one screw on each hinge with a 3½" screw, but be careful not to overtighten them and pull the frame out of square.

4. Nail through the brick molding and into the sheathing (or siding) and framing with 16d casing nails driven every 16".

5. Cut off the shims flush with the framing, using a utility knife. Set all nails with a nail set.

A. Plumb the door jamb, working from the top-down. Fasten through the jamb and each shim pair with a casing nail.

B. Shim the latch jamb, using the gap between the door and the jamb as a gauge. Make sure the gap is consistent.

Homemade Doors & Windows

To make your own door or window, build and install the frame, measure the opening, then build and install the door to fit (or add the glass). Use 1 × lumber for the frame, ripping it to width so it spans the wall section of the rough opening.

You can make a homemade door with almost any rigid board: siding, plywood, lumber, etc. Use the door plans provided in the shed project or create your own design.

For windows, you can use standard plate glass, safety glass (tempered), or Plexiglass™. Plexiglass has more shock-resistance than glass, but it's no less expensive, and it becomes scratched and cloudy over time.

Installing a homemade door or window frame is similar to

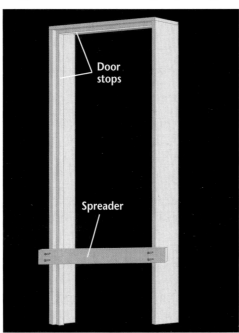

installing a prehung door: center the frame in the rough opening, shim between the jambs and framing, plumb and level the frame, and fasten it through the jamb and shims (see pages 45 to 46). Because a homemade door frame has no threshold to secure the bottom ends of the side jambs, install a temporary 1 × spreader across the jambs to keep the frame square during installation.

To install a homemade door, mount the hinges to the door, then set the door in the frame and hold it against the stops. Insert shims underneath the door and between the door and latch jamb to set even gaps around the door. Mount the hinges to the wall with screws (see page 81).

FLASHING ABOVE DOORS & WINDOWS

Install metal flashing where siding meets trim to help divert water away from doors, windows, and their frames.

*When the siding is installed **after** the trim:*

Nail the flashing to the sheathing so it laps over the trim, then install the siding over the vertical flange of the flashing.

*When the siding is installed **before** the trim:*

1. Set the trim in place above the door or window, then trace along the top edge and ends of the trim (**photo A**).

2. Remove the trim and cut out the siding along the traced lines.

3. Slip the flashing underneath the siding and fasten it with nails driven through the siding (complete the siding nailing).

4. Reinstall the cut-out siding below the flashing—to serve as backing—then install the trim (**photo B**).

A. *Trace along the trim to mark the cutting lines for removing the siding.*

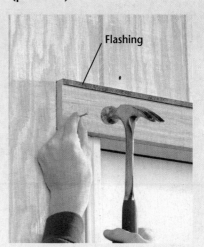

B. *Add the flashing, then install the siding cutout and the trim.*

Photo courtesy of Gardensheds

Projects

Basic Shed

This 8 × 12-ft. shed features a simple gable roof, double doors, and side and rear windows for natural lighting. With full-height walls and doors, there's ample room for storing large items or creating a comfortable work space. An optional wood ramp helps in moving lawn mowers and other heavy equipment.

The shed's simple construction makes it especially adaptable for different uses. For example, you can easily frame in additional windows—to use the shed as a workshop or potting shed—or omit all of the windows and devote the space entirely to secure storage.

The finish materials for the basic shed also are true to its name: asphalt roof shingles, plywood siding, and simple trim details are appropriately practical for this classic outbuilding design. You can purchase prehung doors, like those shown in the illustration below, or build your own using the project plans.

Materials

Description	Quantity/Size	Material
Foundation		
Drainage material	1.4 cu. yd.	Compactible gravel
Skids	3 @ 12'-0"	4 × 4 treated timbers
Floor Framing		
Rim joists	2 @ 12'-0"	2 × 6 pressure-treated
Joists	10 @ 8'-0"	2 × 6 pressure-treated
Floor sheathing	3 sheets, 4 × 8'	¾" tongue-&-groove ext.-grade plywood
Joist clip angles	20	3" × 3" × 3" × 16-gauge galvanized
Wall Framing		
Bottom plates	2 @ 12'-0" 1 @ 8'-0"	2 × 4
Top plates	4 @ 12'-0" 4 @ 8'-0"	2 × 4
Studs	40 @ 92⅝"	2 × 4
Headers	2 @ 10'-0", 2 @ 6'0"	2 × 6
Header spacers	1 @ 9'-0", 1 @ 6'-0"	½" plywood—5" wide
Gable Wall Framing		
Top plates	2 @ 8'-0"	2 × 4
Studs	2 @ 8'-0"	2 × 4
Roof Framing		
Rafters	22 @ 6'-0"	2 × 6
Metal anchors—rafters	10, with nails	Simpson H1
Rafter ties	3 @ 8'-0"	2 × 4
Ridge board	1 @ 14'-0"	2 × 8
Lookouts	1 @ 8'-0"	2 × 6
Subfascia	1 @ 8'-0", 2 @ 10'-0"	2 × 6
Soffit nailers	3 @ 8'-0"	2 × 2
Exterior Finishes		
Plywood siding	10 sheets @ 4 × 9'	⅝" texture 1-11 plywood siding, grooves 8" o.c.
Z-flashing	2 pieces @ 8 ft.	Galvanized—18 gauge
Wall & corner trim	10 @ 10'-0"	1 × 4 S4S cedar
Fascia	8 @ 8'-0"	1 × 8 S4S cedar
Plywood soffits	2 sheets @ 4 × 8'	⅜" cedar or fir plywood
Soffit vents	4 @ 4 × 12"	Louver with bug screen
Flashing (door/window trim)	8 linear ft.	Galvanized—18 gauge
Roofing		
Roof sheathing	6 sheets @ 4 × 8'	½" ext.-grade plywood
Asphalt shingles	150 sq. ft.	250# per square (min.)
15# building paper	150 sq. ft.	
Metal drip edge	2 @ 14'-0", 4 @ 6'-0"	Galvanized metal
Roof vents (optional)	2 units	

Description	Quantity/Size	Material
Door		
Frame	2 @ 8'-0", 1 @ 6'-0"	¾ × 4¼" (actual) S4S cedar
Stops	2 @ 8'-0", 1 @ 6'-0"	1 × 2 S4S cedar
Panel material	12 @ 8'-0"	1 × 6 T&G V-joint S4S cedar
Z-brace	4 @ 6'-0"	1 × 6 S4S cedar
Construction adhesive	1 tube	
Exterior trim	2 @ 8'-0", 1 @ 6'-0"	1 × 4 S4S cedar
Interior trim (optional)	2 @ 8'-0", 1 @ 6'-0"	1 × 2 S4S cedar
Strap hinges	6, with screws	Exterior hinges
Windows		
Frames	5 @ 6'-0"	¾ × 4¼" (actual) S4S cedar
Mullion	1 @ 3'-0"	2 × 4 S4S cedar
Stops	10 @ 6'-0"	1 × 2 S4S cedar
Glazing tape	30 linear ft.	Glazing tape
Glass	3 pieces—field measure	¼" clear, tempered
Window muntins (optional)	3 @ 8'-0"	1 × 1 S4S cedar
Exterior trim	5 @ 8'-0"	1 × 4 S4S cedar
Interior trim (optional)	5 @ 8'-0"	1 × 2 S4S cedar
Ramp (Optional)		
Pads	2 @ 6'-0"	2 × 8 pressure-treated
Stringers	1 @ 8'-0"	2 × 8 pressure-treated
Decking	7 @ 6'-0"	2 × 4 pressure-treated
Fasteners		
16d common nails	16 lbs.	
10d common nails	1 lb.	
10d galvanized casing nails	1 lb.	
8d common nails	½ lb.	
8d box nails	3 lbs.	
8d galvanized box nails	1½ lbs.	
8d galvanized finish nails	7 lbs.	
3d galvanized box nails	¼ lb.	
⅞" galvanized roofing nails	2 lbs.	
1½" joist hanger nails	80 nails	
1¼" wood screws	70 screws	
3½" deck screws	12 screws	
3" deck screws	50 screws	
2½" deck screws	40 screws	
1¼" deck screws	30 screws	
Silicone-latex caulk	1 tube	

FRONT FRAMING ELEVATION

LEFT SIDE FRAMING ELEVATION

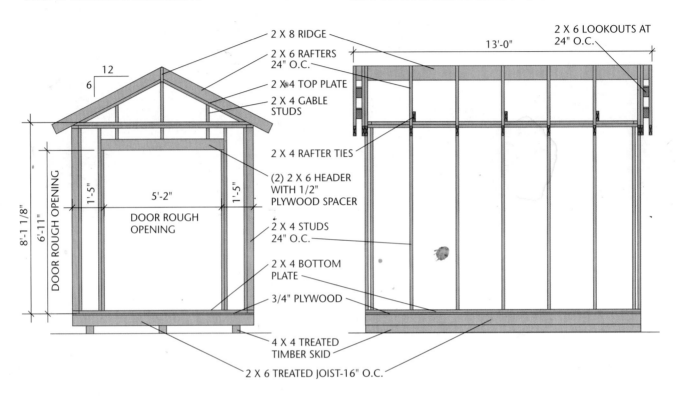

2 X 8 RIDGE

2 X 6 RAFTERS 24" O.C.

2 X 4 TOP PLATE

2 X 4 GABLE STUDS

2 X 4 RAFTER TIES

(2) 2 X 6 HEADER WITH 1/2" PLYWOOD SPACER

2 X 4 STUDS 24" O.C.

2 X 4 BOTTOM PLATE

3/4" PLYWOOD

4 X 4 TREATED TIMBER SKID

2 X 6 TREATED JOIST-16" O.C.

2 X 6 LOOKOUTS AT 24" O.C.

13'-0"

12
6

8'-1 1/8"

6'-11"

DOOR ROUGH OPENING

1'-5"

5'-2"

DOOR ROUGH OPENING

1'-5"

REAR FRAMING ELEVATION

RIGHT SIDE FRAMING ELEVATION

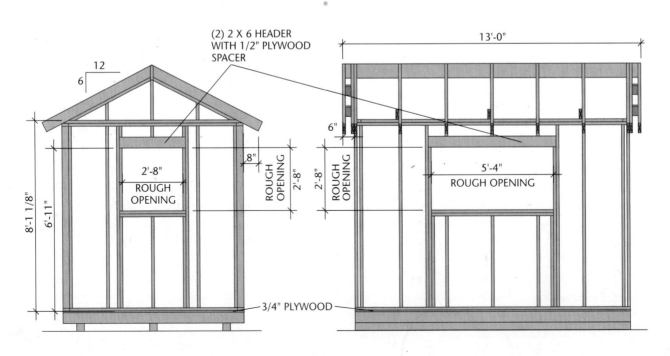

(2) 2 X 6 HEADER WITH 1/2" PLYWOOD SPACER

12
6

8'-1 1/8"

6'-11"

2'-8"
ROUGH OPENING

8"

ROUGH OPENING

2'-8"

3/4" PLYWOOD

13'-0"

6"

6"

ROUGH OPENING

2'-8"

5'-4"
ROUGH OPENING

BUILDING SECTION

2 X 8 RIDGE BOARD

ASPHALT SHINGLES OVER
15# BUILDING PAPER &
1/2" PLYWOOD SHEATHING

12
6

2 X 6 RAFTERS
24" O.C.

2 X 6 SUBFASCIA

2 X 4 RAFTER
TIES - 48" O.C.

1 X 8 FASCIA

8"

(2) 2 X 6 HEADER
W/ 1/2" PLYWOOD
SPACER

8'-1 1/8"

2 X 4 STUDS
24" O.C.

HOMEMADE
WINDOW

2 X 4 BOTTOM
PLATE

TEXTURE 1-11
PLYWOOD SIDING

GRADE

4 X 4 TREATED
TIMBER SKID

3/4" PLYWOOD

2 X 6 TREATED
JOIST - 16" O.C.

RAFTER TEMPLATE

12
6

5'-3"

2 X 6 RAFTER

1 3/4"

3 1/2"

7 1/2"

FLOOR FRAMING PLAN

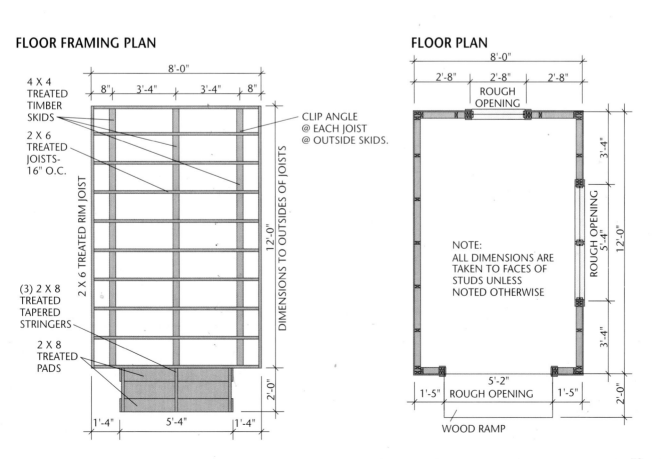

4 X 4
TREATED
TIMBER
SKIDS

2 X 6
TREATED
JOISTS-
16" O.C.

2 X 6 TREATED RIM JOIST

(3) 2 X 8
TREATED
TAPERED
STRINGERS

2 X 8
TREATED
PADS

8'-0"

8"   3'-4"   3'-4"   8"

CLIP ANGLE
@ EACH JOIST
@ OUTSIDE SKIDS.

DIMENSIONS TO OUTSIDES OF JOISTS

12'-0"

2'-0"

1'-4"   5'-4"   1'-4"

FLOOR PLAN

8'-0"

2'-8"   2'-8"   2'-8"

ROUGH
OPENING

3'-4"

ROUGH OPENING

5'-4"

12'-0"

NOTE:
ALL DIMENSIONS ARE
TAKEN TO FACES OF
STUDS UNLESS
NOTED OTHERWISE

3'-4"

2'-0"

1'-5"   ROUGH OPENING   1'-5"

5'-2"

WOOD RAMP

FRONT ELEVATION

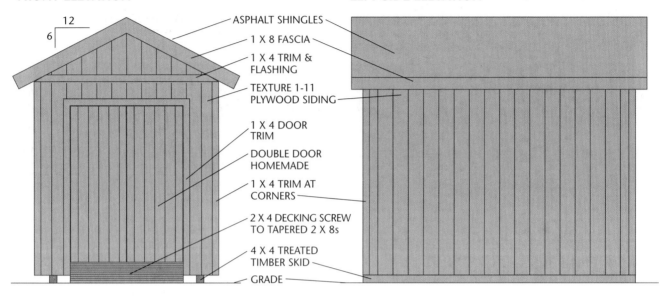

12
6

ASPHALT SHINGLES

1 X 8 FASCIA

1 X 4 TRIM & FLASHING

TEXTURE 1-11 PLYWOOD SIDING

1 X 4 DOOR TRIM

DOUBLE DOOR HOMEMADE

1 X 4 TRIM AT CORNERS

2 X 4 DECKING SCREW TO TAPERED 2 X 8s

4 X 4 TREATED TIMBER SKID

GRADE

LEFT SIDE ELEVATION

REAR ELEVATION

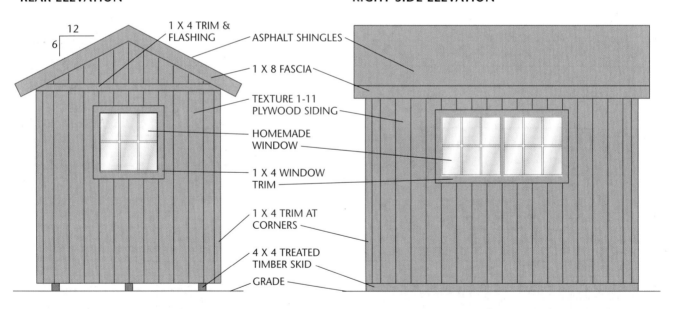

12
6

1 X 4 TRIM & FLASHING

1 X 4 WINDOW TRIM

1 X 4 TRIM AT CORNERS

4 X 4 TREATED TIMBER SKID

GRADE

RIGHT SIDE ELEVATION

ASPHALT SHINGLES

1 X 8 FASCIA

TEXTURE 1-11 PLYWOOD SIDING

HOMEMADE WINDOW

HORIZONTAL TRIM DETAIL

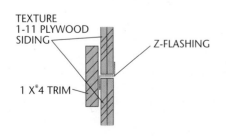

TEXTURE 1-11 PLYWOOD SIDING

Z-FLASHING

1 X 4 TRIM

DOOR JAMB DETAIL

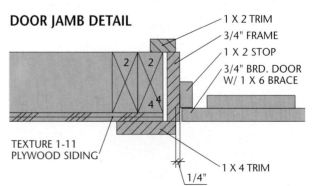

1 X 2 TRIM

3/4" FRAME

1 X 2 STOP

3/4" BRD. DOOR W/ 1 X 6 BRACE

2   2

4 4

TEXTURE 1-11 PLYWOOD SIDING

1 X 4 TRIM

1/4"

GABLE OVERHANG DETAIL

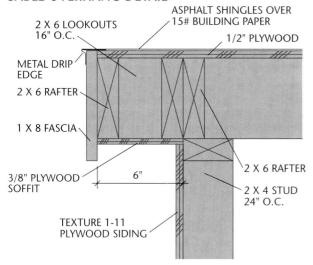

2 X 6 LOOKOUTS 16" O.C.

ASPHALT SHINGLES OVER 15# BUILDING PAPER

1/2" PLYWOOD

METAL DRIP EDGE

2 X 6 RAFTER

1 X 8 FASCIA

3/8" PLYWOOD SOFFIT

6"

2 X 6 RAFTER

2 X 4 STUD 24" O.C.

TEXTURE 1-11 PLYWOOD SIDING

EAVE DETAIL

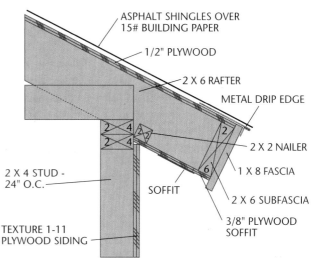

ASPHALT SHINGLES OVER 15# BUILDING PAPER

1/2" PLYWOOD

2 X 6 RAFTER

METAL DRIP EDGE

2 X 2 NAILER

1 X 8 FASCIA

2 X 6 SUBFASCIA

3/8" PLYWOOD SOFFIT

SOFFIT

2 X 4 STUD - 24" O.C.

TEXTURE 1-11 PLYWOOD SIDING

WINDOW JAMB DETAIL

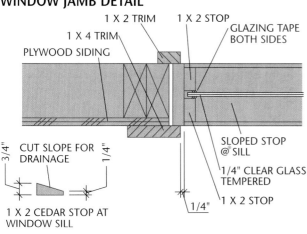

1 X 2 TRIM

1 X 2 STOP

1 X 4 TRIM

GLAZING TAPE BOTH SIDES

PLYWOOD SIDING

SLOPED STOP @ SILL

1/4" CLEAR GLASS TEMPERED

1 X 2 STOP

3/4"

1/4"

CUT SLOPE FOR DRAINAGE

1 X 2 CEDAR STOP AT WINDOW SILL

1/4"

RAMP DETAIL (OPTIONAL)

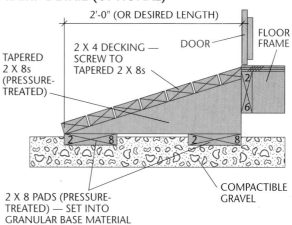

2'-0" (OR DESIRED LENGTH)

2 X 4 DECKING — SCREW TO TAPERED 2 X 8s

DOOR

FLOOR FRAME

TAPERED 2 X 8s (PRESSURE-TREATED)

2

6

2   8

2   8

2 X 8 PADS (PRESSURE-TREATED) — SET INTO GRANULAR BASE MATERIAL

COMPACTIBLE GRAVEL

DOOR ELEVATIONS

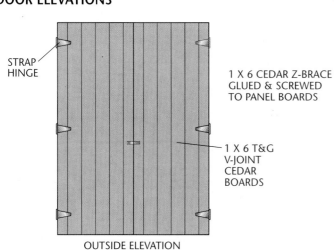

STRAP HINGE

1 X 6 T&G V-JOINT CEDAR BOARDS

OUTSIDE ELEVATION

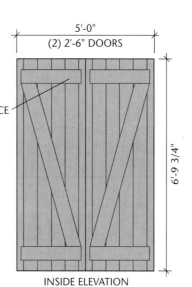

5'-0"

(2) 2'-6" DOORS

1 X 6 CEDAR Z-BRACE GLUED & SCREWED TO PANEL BOARDS

6'-9 3/4"

INSIDE ELEVATION

55

BUILDING THE BASIC SHED

Step A: Build the Foundation & Floor Frame

1. Excavate the building site and add a 4" layer of compactible gravel. If desired, add an extension to the base for the optional wood ramp. Tamp the gravel thoroughly, making sure it is flat and level.

2. Cut three 4 × 4 treated timber skids at 144". Arrange and level the skids on the gravel bed, following the FLOOR FRAMING PLAN, on page 53.

3. Cut two 2 × 6 rim joists at 144" and ten joists at 93". Mark the joist layout onto the rim joists, following the plan. Assemble frame with 16d galv. common nails; be sure to check each joist for crowning and install it with the crowned edge up.

4. Set the floor frame on top of the skids and measure the diagonals to make sure it's square. Install metal clip angles at each joist along the two outer skids, using 1½" joist hanger nails and 16d galv. common nails, and toenail each joist to the center skid with 16d galv. nails.

5. Install the tongue-and-groove floor sheathing, starting with a full sheet at one corner of the frame. Use 8d galv. nails driven every 6" along the edges and every 12" in the field.

Step B: Frame the Walls

1. Snap chalk lines on the floor for the wall plates.

2. Cut the 2 × 4 wall plates: four at 144" for the side walls and four at 89" for the front and back walls.

3. Mark the stud layouts onto the plates following the FLOOR PLAN, on page 53.

4. Cut twenty-seven studs at 92⅝", and cut six at 81½" to serve as jack studs.

5. Build three headers with 2 × 6s and ½" plywood: one at 65" for the door opening, one at 67" for the right side window, and one at 35" for the rear window.

6. Assemble, raise, and brace the walls one at a time, then add the double top plates.

Step C: Frame the Roof

1. Cut two pattern rafters, following the RAFTER TEMPLATE, on page 53. Test-fit the rafters using a 2 × 8 spacer block, then cut the remaining twelve common rafters. Cut eight rafters for the gable end overhangs—these do not have bird's mouth cuts.

2. Cut the 2 × 8 ridge board at 156". Draw the rafter layout onto the top plates and ridge board, using 16" on-center spacing. The outsides of the outer common rafters should be 6" from the ends of the ridge board.

3. Install the rafters. Reinforce the rafter-wall connection with metal anchors—install them on all but the outer common rafters.

A. *Secure the joists to the outer skids with angles. Drive hanger nails into the joists and 16d nails into the skids.*

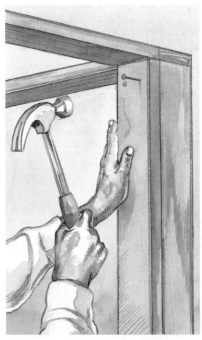

B. *Frame and raise the walls, then fasten adjacent walls together at the corner studs.*

C. *Fasten the bottom ends of the common rafters to the wall plates with metal anchors.*

4. Cut three 2 × 4 rafter ties at 96", and clip the top outer corners so they won't project above the rafters. Position each tie next to a pair of rafters as shown in the FRAMING ELEVATIONS on page 52. Facenail each tie end to the rafter with three 10d nails, then toenail each tie end to the top wall plate with two 8d nails.

5. Cut the gable-wall plates to reach from the ridge to the wall plates. Install the plates with their outside edges flush with the outer common rafters. Cut and install the gable studs, following the FRAMING ELEVATIONS, on page 52.

Step D: Build the Gable Overhangs

1. Cut twelve 2 × 6 lookouts at 3". Endnail the lookouts to each of the inner overhang rafters, using 16" on-center spacing (see the GABLE OVER-HANG DETAIL, on page 55).

2. Facenail the inner overhang rafters to the outer common rafters with 10d nails.

3. Fasten the outer overhang rafters to the ridge and lookouts, using 16d nails.

Step E: Install the Fascia, Sheathing & Roofing

1. Cut and install the 2 × 6 subfascia along the eaves (see the EAVE DETAIL, on page 55). Keep the ends flush with the outsides of the overhang rafters, and the bottom edges flush with the bottom rafter edges; use 16d nails.

2. Install the 1 × 8 fascia along the gable over-hangs, then along the eaves, holding it ½" above the rafters so it will be flush with the sheathing; use 6d galv. finish nails.

3. Install the ½" plywood sheathing, starting at a lower corner of the roof; use 8d box nails driven every 6" along the edges and every 12" in the field of the sheets.

4. Attach metal drip edge along the eaves, then apply 15# building paper over the sheathing. Add drip edge along the gable ends, over the paper.

5. Install the asphalt shingles, starting at the eave edge. If desired, install roof vents (see page 37).

Step F: Install the Soffits & Siding

1. Cut twelve 2 × 2 nailers to fit between the rafters, as shown in the EAVE DETAIL, on page 55. Fasten the nailers between the rafters with 10d facenails or 8d toenails.

2. Rip the ⅜" plywood soffit panels to fit between the wall framing and the fascia. Fasten the soffits to the rafters with 3d galv. box nails.

3. Cut holes for four soffit vents: locate one vent in each of the two outer rafter bays, along the eave, on both sides of the building. Install the soffit vents.

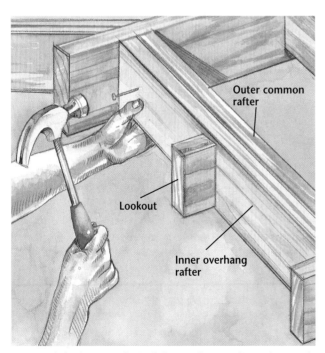

D. *Attach lookouts to four of the overhang rafters, then nail the overhang rafters to the outer common rafters.*

Outer common rafter

Lookout

Inner overhang rafter

E. *Install the plywood roof sheathing after installing the fascia. Nail every 6" at the edges and every 12" in the field.*

F. *Rip the soffit panels to fit between the wall plates and fascia. Fasten the panels to the nailers, rafters, and subfascia.*

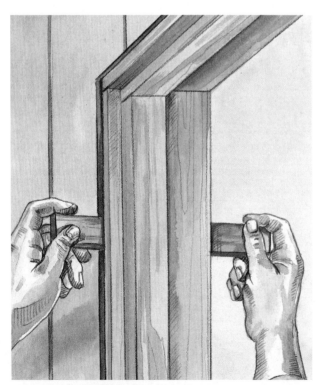

G. *Use pairs of tapered shims to plumb and level the door frame in the rough opening.*

4. Install the plywood siding, using 8d galv. finish nails. Butt the top edges of the siding against the soffits. Don't nail the siding to the rear-window and door headers in this step. At the gable ends, install Z-flashing along the top edge of siding, then continue the siding up to the soffits.

Note: Along the side walls, 8-ft. siding will cover the floor plywood by about ½" (this is necessary); if you want the siding to cover the floor framing, use 4 × 9-ft. sheets.

Step G: Build & Install the Doors

1. Cut out the bottom plate from the door opening.

2. Cut the door frame pieces from ¾ × 4½" (actual dimension) cedar: cut the head jamb at 61¼" and the side jambs at 81⅞". Assemble the frame by screwing through the head jamb and into the side jambs with 2½" deck screws.

3. Cut 1 × 2 stops and install them inside the jambs with 1¼" deck screws or 3d galv. finish nails. If the doors will swing out, install the stops 2¼" from the outside edges of the frame; if they'll swing in, install the stops 2¼" from the inside edges.

4. Install the door frame in the rough opening, using shims and 10d galv. casing nails (see page 47). Make sure the frame is square and plumb.

5. Cut twelve pieces of 1 × 6 tongue-&-groove boards at 81¾". For each door, fit together six boards with their ends flush, then mark the two end boards for trimming so that the total width is 30". Trim the end boards.

6. Cut the Z-brace boards following the DOOR ELEVATIONS, on page 55. Lay the doors on a flat surface and attach the brace boards using construction adhesive and 1¼" wood screws.

7. Install the hinges and hang the door, using shims to set the gaps at the bottom and top of each door (see page 81).

8. Install flashing above the door (see page 47), nail-off the siding, then install the 1 × 4 door trim, using 8d galv. finish nails.

Step H: Build & Install the Windows & Trim

Note: If you've bought prehung windows for the shed, install them following the manufacturer's directions (see pages 45 to 47). To build homemade windows, use the following directions.

1. For each window, cut the ¾" × 4¼" frame stock to form a rectangular frame with outer dimensions that are ½" shorter and narrower than the rough opening. Assemble the frame with 2½" deck screws. Cut and install a 2 × 4 mullion in the center of the frame for the side-wall window.

2. Install each window frame in its rough opening, using shims and a level to make sure the frame is plumb and level and the jambs are straight. Fasten the frame with 10d galv. casing nails.

3. Cut the 1 × 2 stops. Bevel the outer sill stops as shown in the WINDOW JAMB DETAIL, on page 55. Attach the inner stops with 6d galv. finish nails. Order the glass to fit.

4. Install the glass and outer stops, applying glazing tape to the stops on both sides of the glass. Install the 1 × 4 window trim.

5. Install the horizontal 1 × 4 trim as shown in the ELEVATIONS, on page 54. Fasten the trim with 8d galv. finish nails.

6. Install the 1 × 4 corner trim so that it butts against the horizontal trim and extends to the bottom edges of the siding.

7. Caulk along all trim joints, where trim meets siding, and around the door and window trim.

Step I: Build the Ramp (Optional)

Determining the width and length (and thus the slope) of the ramp is up to you, but here is the basic construction procedure:

1. Determine the best slope for the ramp using boards or plywood set on the ground and the shed floor. Mark the ground to represent the end of the ramp.

2. Cut two 2 × 8 pads to the full width of the ramp.

3. Measure the distance from the ground to the shed floor; subtract 2" from that dimension to get the height of the tapered stringers.

4. Use the ground marking to determine the length of the stringers—be sure to account for the 1½" thickness of the decking. Cut the tapered stringers from 2 × 8 lumber: cut one for each end and one for every 16" to 24" in between.

5. Attach the pads to the stringers with 16d galv. nails driven through the bottom faces of the pads and into the stringers.

6. Cut 2 × 4s for the ramp decking—the number needed depends on the length of the sloping sides of the stringers. Allow for a ⅛" gap between decking boards when calculating the number needed.

7. Attach the decking boards to the supports with 16d galv. nails or 3" deck screws, maintaining a ⅛" gap between boards.

8. Set the ramp in place against the shed and fasten it by toenailing through the end stringers and top decking board with 3½" deck screws.

H. *Assemble the window frames with screws. Add a 2 × 4 mullion in the center of the side window frame.*

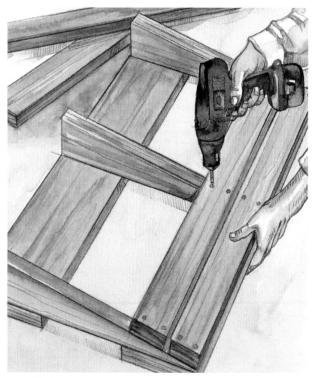

I. *Build the ramp with pressure-treated 2 × 8s and 2 × 4s, following the plan's size or building it to a custom size.*

Lawn-tractor Garage

Following classic barn designs, this 12 × 12-ft. garage has several features that make it a versatile storage shed. The garage's floor is a poured concrete slab with a thickened edge that allows it to serve also as the building's foundation. Designed for economy and durability, the floor can support a lawn tractor, large stationary tools, or other heavy equipment. See pages 18 to 21 for detailed information on the foundation and how to build it.

For easy access with large items, there's a full-width sectional garage door. The door opening is sized for an 8-ft.-wide × 7-ft.-tall door, but you can buy any size or style—just make sure to get the door before you start framing.

Another functional (and equally aesthetic) feature of this shed is its gambrel roof, a style commonly used for barns because it maximizes the usable interior space. Beneath the roof is a sizable storage attic—a 315 cubic-ft. space with its own double-doors above the garage door.

Materials

Description	Quantity/Size	Material
Foundation		
Drainage material	1.75 cu. yds.	Compactible gravel
Concrete slab	2.5 cu. yds.	3,000 psi concrete
Mesh	144 sq. ft.	6 × 6", W1.4 × W1.4 welded wire mesh
Wall Framing		
Bottom plates	4 @ 12'-0"	2 × 4 pressure-treated
Top Plates	8 @ 12'-0"	2 × 4
Studs	47 @ 92⅝"	2 × 4
Headers	2 @ 10'-0", 2 @ 6'-0"	2 × 8
Header spacers	1 @ 9'-0", 1 @ 6'-0"	½" plywood—7" wide
Angle braces	1 @ 4'-0"	2 × 4
Gable Wall Framing		
Plates	2 @ 10'-0"	2 × 4
Studs	7 @ 10'-0"	2 × 4
Header	2 @ 6'-0"	2 × 6
Header spacer	1 @ 5'-0"	½" plywood—5" wide
Attic Floor		
Joists	10 @ 12'-0"	2 × 6
Floor sheathing	3 sheets @ 4 × 8'	¾" tongue-&-groove ext.-grade plywood
Kneewall Framing		
Bottom plates	2 @ 12'-0"	2 × 4
Top plates	4 @ 12'-0"	2 × 4
Studs	8 @ 10'-0"	2 × 4
Nailers	2 @ 14'-0"	2 × 8
Roof Framing		
Rafters	28 @ 10'-0"	2 × 4
Metal anchors—rafters	20, with nails	Simpson H2.5
Collar ties	2 @ 6'-0"	2 × 4
Ridge board	1 @ 14'-0"	2 × 6
Lookouts	1 @ 10'-0"	2 × 4
Soffit ledgers	2 @ 14'-0"	2 × 4
Soffit blocking	6 @ 8'-0"	2 × 4
Exterior Finishes		
Plywood siding	14 sheets @ 4 × 8'	⅝" texture 1-11 plywood, grooves 8" o. c.
Z-flashing—siding	2 pieces @ 12'-0"	Galvanized 18-gauge
Horizontal wall trim	2 @ 12'-0"	1 × 4 S4S cedar
Corner trim	8 @ 8'-0"	1 × 4 S4S cedar
Fascia	6 @ 10'-0", 2 @ 8'-0"	1 × 6 S4S cedar
Subfascia	4 @ 8'-0"	1 × 4 pine
Plywood soffits	1 sheet @ 10'-0"	⅜" cedar or fir plywood
Soffit vents	4 @ 4 × 12"	Louver w/bug screen
Flashing—garage door	1 @ 10'-0"	Galvanized 18-gauge

Description	Quantity/Size	Material
Roofing		
Roof sheathing	12 sheets @ 4 × 8'	½" plywood
Shingles	3 squares	250# per square (min.)
15# building paper	300 sq. ft.	
Metal drip edge	2 @ 14'-0", 2 @ 12'-0"	Galvanized metal
Roof vents (optional)	2 units	
Window		
Frame	3 @ 6'-0"	¾ × 4" (actual) S4S cedar
Stops	4 @ 8'-0"	1 × 2 S4S cedar
Glazing tape	30 linear ft.	
Glass	1 piece—field measure	¼"clear, tempered
Exterior trim	3 @ 6'-0"	1 × 4 S4S cedar
Interior trim (optional)	3 @ 6'-0"	1 × 2 S4S cedar
Door		
Frame	2 @ 8'-0"	1 × 6 S4S cedar
Door sill	1 @ 6'-0"	1 × 6 S4S cedar
Stops	1 @ 8'-0", 1 @ 6'-0"	1 × 2 S4S cedar
Panel material	4 @ 8'-0"	1 × 8 T&G V-joint S4S cedar
Door X-brace/panel trim	4 @ 6'-0", 2 @ 8'-0"	1 × 4 S4S cedar
Exterior trim	1 @ 8'-0", 1 @ 6'-0"	1 × 4 S4S cedar
Interior trim (optional)	1 @ 8'-0", 1 @ 6'-0"	1 × 2 S4S cedar
Strap hinges	4	
Garage Door		
Frame	3 @ 8'-0"	1 × 8 S4S cedar
Door	1 @ 8'-0" × 6'-8"	Sectional flush door w/2" track
Rails	2 @ 8'-0"	2 × 6
Trim	3 @ 8'-0"	1 × 4 S4S cedar
Fasteners		
Anchor bolts	16	⅜" × 8", with washers & nuts
16d galvanized common nails	2 lbs.	
16d common nails	17 lbs.	
10d common nails	2 lbs.	
10d galvanized casing nails	1 lb.	
8d common nails	3 lbs.	
8d galvanized finish nails	6 lbs.	
8d box nails	6 lbs.	
6d galvanized finish nails	20 nails	
3d galvanized box nails	½ lb.	
⅞" galvanized roofing nails	2½ lbs.	
2½" deck screws	24 screws	
1¼" wood screws	48 screws	
Construction adhesive	2 tubes	
Silicone-latex caulk	2 tubes	

FRONT FRAMING ELEVATION

LEFT SIDE FRAMING ELEVATION

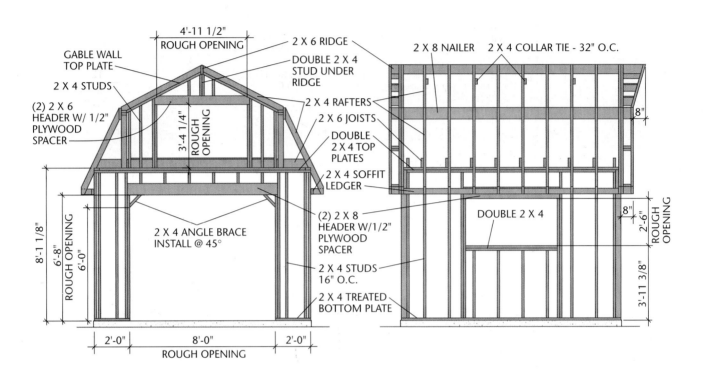

4'-11 1/2"
ROUGH OPENING

2 X 6 RIDGE

DOUBLE 2 X 4
STUD UNDER
RIDGE

GABLE WALL
TOP PLATE

2 X 4 STUDS

(2) 2 X 6
HEADER W/ 1/2"
PLYWOOD
SPACER

3'-4 1/4"
ROUGH OPENING

2 X 4 RAFTERS

2 X 6 JOISTS

DOUBLE
2 X 4 TOP
PLATES

2 X 4 SOFFIT
LEDGER

(2) 2 X 8
HEADER W/1/2"
PLYWOOD
SPACER

2 X 4 ANGLE BRACE
INSTALL @ 45°

2 X 4 STUDS
16" O.C.

2 X 4 TREATED
BOTTOM PLATE

8'-1 1/8"

6'-8"
ROUGH OPENING

6'-0"

2'-0"   8'-0"   2'-0"
ROUGH OPENING

2 X 8 NAILER   2 X 4 COLLAR TIE - 32" O.C.

8"

DOUBLE 2 X 4

8"
2'-6"
ROUGH OPENING

3'-11 3/8"

REAR FRAMING ELEVATION

RIGHT SIDE FRAMING ELEVATION

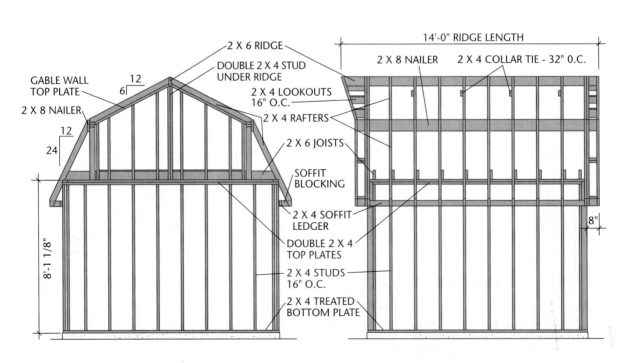

2 X 6 RIDGE

DOUBLE 2 X 4 STUD
UNDER RIDGE

GABLE WALL
TOP PLATE

2 X 8 NAILER

12
6

12
24

2 X 4 LOOKOUTS
16" O.C.

2 X 4 RAFTERS

2 X 6 JOISTS

SOFFIT
BLOCKING

2 X 4 SOFFIT
LEDGER

DOUBLE 2 X 4
TOP PLATES

2 X 4 STUDS
16" O.C.

2 X 4 TREATED
BOTTOM PLATE

8'-1 1/8"

14'-0" RIDGE LENGTH

2 X 8 NAILER   2 X 4 COLLAR TIE - 32" O.C.

8"

BUILDING SECTION

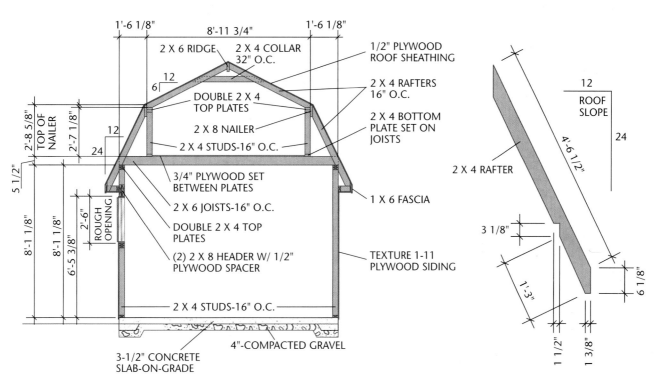

- 1'-6 1/8"
- 8'-11 3/4"
- 1'-6 1/8"
- 2 X 6 RIDGE
- 2 X 4 COLLAR 32" O.C.
- 1/2" PLYWOOD ROOF SHEATHING
- 6 | 12
- 2 X 4 RAFTERS 16" O.C.
- DOUBLE 2 X 4 TOP PLATES
- 2 X 4 BOTTOM PLATE SET ON JOISTS
- 2 X 8 NAILER
- 2'-8 5/8" TOP OF NAILER
- 2'-7 1/8"
- 12 | 24
- 2 X 4 STUDS-16" O.C.
- 5 1/2"
- 3/4" PLYWOOD SET BETWEEN PLATES
- 1 X 6 FASCIA
- 8'-1 1/8"
- 8'-1 1/8"
- ROUGH OPENING
- 2'-6"
- 6'-5 3/8"
- 2 X 6 JOISTS-16" O.C.
- DOUBLE 2 X 4 TOP PLATES
- (2) 2 X 8 HEADER W/ 1/2" PLYWOOD SPACER
- TEXTURE 1-11 PLYWOOD SIDING
- 2 X 4 STUDS-16" O.C.
- 4"-COMPACTED GRAVEL
- 3-1/2" CONCRETE SLAB-ON-GRADE

RAFTER TEMPLATE-LOWER RAFTER

- 12 | ROOF SLOPE | 24
- 4'-6 1/2"
- 2 X 4 RAFTER
- 3 1/8"
- 1'-3"
- 6 1/8"
- 1 1/2"
- 1 3/8"

FLOOR PLAN

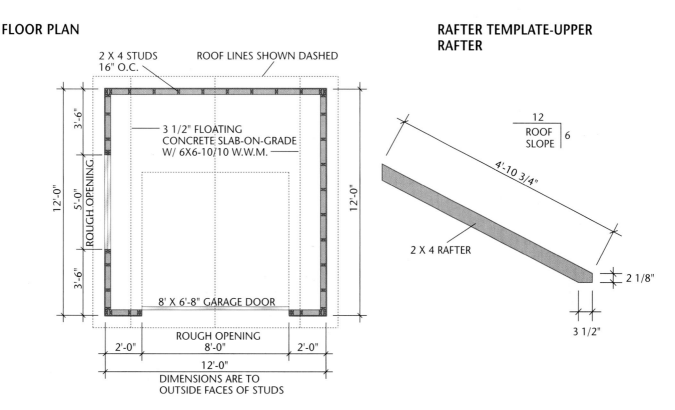

- 2 X 4 STUDS 16" O.C.
- ROOF LINES SHOWN DASHED
- 3'-6"
- 3 1/2" FLOATING CONCRETE SLAB-ON-GRADE W/ 6X6-10/10 W.W.M.
- 12'-0"
- 5'-0"
- ROUGH OPENING
- 12'-0"
- 3'-6"
- 8' X 6'-8" GARAGE DOOR
- 2'-0"
- ROUGH OPENING 8'-0"
- 2'-0"
- 12'-0"
- DIMENSIONS ARE TO OUTSIDE FACES OF STUDS

RAFTER TEMPLATE-UPPER RAFTER

- 12 | ROOF SLOPE | 6
- 4'-10 3/4"
- 2 X 4 RAFTER
- 2 1/8"
- 3 1/2"

FRONT ELEVATION

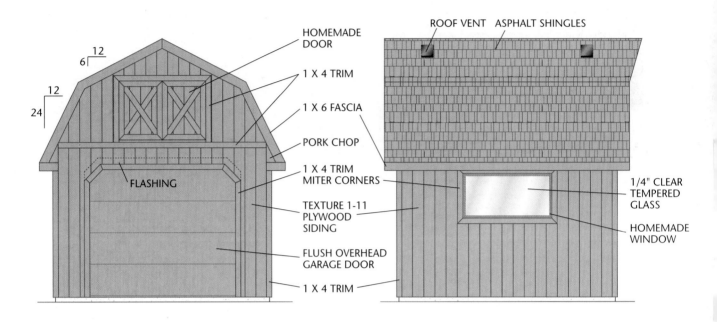

HOMEMADE DOOR

1 X 4 TRIM

1 X 6 FASCIA

PORK CHOP

1 X 4 TRIM
MITER CORNERS

TEXTURE 1-11 PLYWOOD SIDING

FLUSH OVERHEAD GARAGE DOOR

1 X 4 TRIM

FLASHING

12
6⌐

12
24

LEFT SIDE ELEVATION

ROOF VENT   ASPHALT SHINGLES

1/4" CLEAR TEMPERED GLASS

HOMEMADE WINDOW

REAR ELEVATION

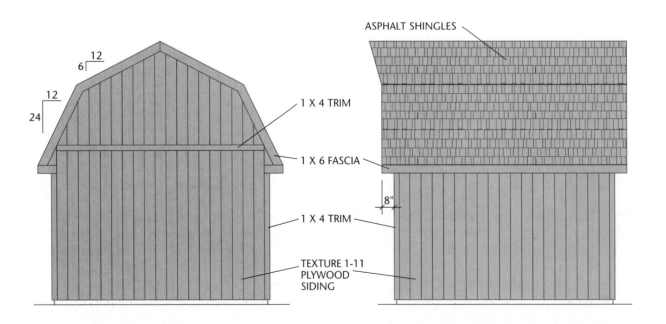

12
6⌐

12
24

1 X 4 TRIM

1 X 6 FASCIA

1 X 4 TRIM

TEXTURE 1-11 PLYWOOD SIDING

RIGHT SIDE ELEVATION

ASPHALT SHINGLES

8"

GABLE OVERHANG DETAIL

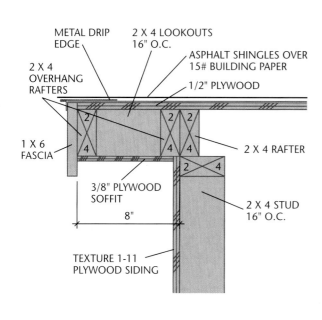

METAL DRIP EDGE

2 X 4 LOOKOUTS 16" O.C.

ASPHALT SHINGLES OVER 15# BUILDING PAPER

2 X 4 OVERHANG RAFTERS

1/2" PLYWOOD

1 X 6 FASCIA

2 X 4 RAFTER

3/8" PLYWOOD SOFFIT

8"

2 X 4 STUD 16" O.C.

TEXTURE 1-11 PLYWOOD SIDING

GABLE OVERHANG RAFTER DETAILS

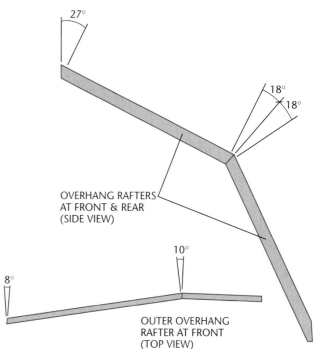

27°

18°
18°

OVERHANG RAFTERS AT FRONT & REAR (SIDE VIEW)

10°

8°

OUTER OVERHANG RAFTER AT FRONT (TOP VIEW)

EAVE DETAIL

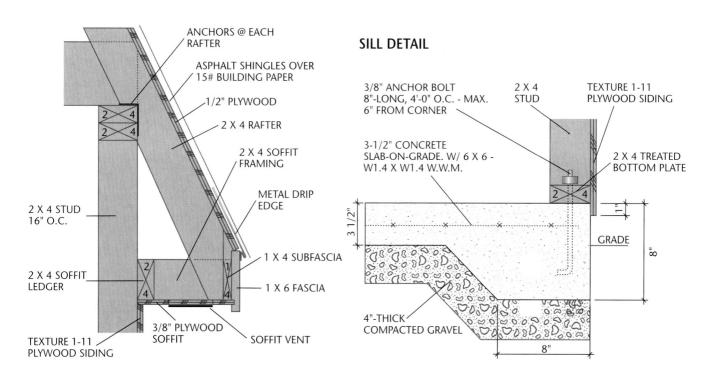

ANCHORS @ EACH RAFTER

ASPHALT SHINGLES OVER 15# BUILDING PAPER

1/2" PLYWOOD

2 X 4 RAFTER

2 X 4 SOFFIT FRAMING

METAL DRIP EDGE

2 X 4 STUD 16" O.C.

2 X 4 SOFFIT LEDGER

1 X 4 SUBFASCIA

1 X 6 FASCIA

TEXTURE 1-11 PLYWOOD SIDING

3/8" PLYWOOD SOFFIT

SOFFIT VENT

SILL DETAIL

3/8" ANCHOR BOLT 8"-LONG, 4'-0" O.C. - MAX. 6" FROM CORNER

2 X 4 STUD

TEXTURE 1-11 PLYWOOD SIDING

3-1/2" CONCRETE SLAB-ON-GRADE. W/ 6 X 6 - W1.4 X W1.4 W.W.M.

2 X 4 TREATED BOTTOM PLATE

3 1/2"

1"

GRADE

8"

4"-THICK COMPACTED GRAVEL

8"

ATTIC DOOR ELEVATION

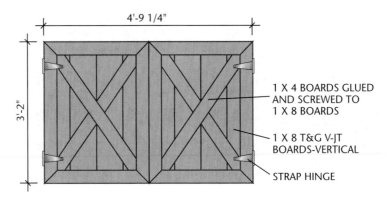

4'-9 1/4"

3'-2"

1 X 4 BOARDS GLUED AND SCREWED TO 1 X 8 BOARDS

1 X 8 T&G V-JT BOARDS-VERTICAL

STRAP HINGE

ATTIC DOOR JAMB DETAIL

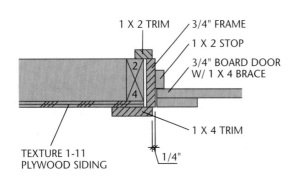

1 X 2 TRIM

3/4" FRAME

1 X 2 STOP

3/4" BOARD DOOR W/ 1 X 4 BRACE

1 X 4 TRIM

TEXTURE 1-11 PLYWOOD SIDING

1/4"

GARAGE DOOR TRIM DETAIL

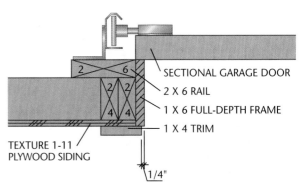

SECTIONAL GARAGE DOOR

2 X 6 RAIL

1 X 6 FULL-DEPTH FRAME

1 X 4 TRIM

TEXTURE 1-11 PLYWOOD SIDING

1/4"

ATTIC DOOR SILL DETAIL

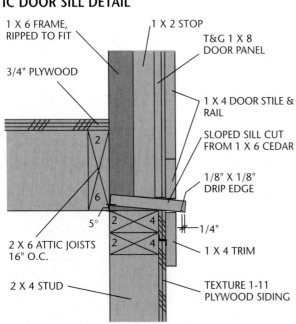

1 X 6 FRAME, RIPPED TO FIT

3/4" PLYWOOD

1 X 2 STOP

T&G 1 X 8 DOOR PANEL

1 X 4 DOOR STILE & RAIL

SLOPED SILL CUT FROM 1 X 6 CEDAR

1/8" X 1/8" DRIP EDGE

1/4"

2 X 6 ATTIC JOISTS 16" O.C.

5°

1 X 4 TRIM

2 X 4 STUD

TEXTURE 1-11 PLYWOOD SIDING

WINDOW JAMB DETAIL

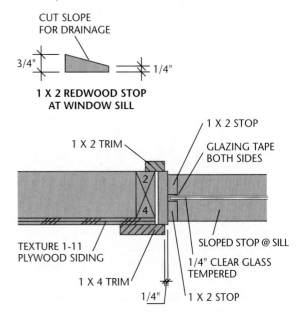

CUT SLOPE FOR DRAINAGE

3/4"

1/4"

1 X 2 REDWOOD STOP AT WINDOW SILL

1 X 2 TRIM

1 X 2 STOP

GLAZING TAPE BOTH SIDES

TEXTURE 1-11 PLYWOOD SIDING

1 X 4 TRIM

1/4"

SLOPED STOP @ SILL

1/4" CLEAR GLASS TEMPERED

1 X 2 STOP

BUILDING THE LAWN-TRACTOR GARAGE

Step A: Pour the Slab Foundation

1. Follow the steps on pages 18 to 21 to prepare the building site, build the concrete form, and pour the slab. The top of the slab should sit 4" above grade and measure exactly 144" × 144". Reinforce the slab internally with welded wire mesh.

2. After floating the concrete, set ⅜" × 8" J-bolts into the slab, 1¾" from the outer edges; install a bolt 6" from each corner and every 4 ft. in between (do not add bolts inside the garage door rough opening). The bolts should protrude from the concrete 2½". Let the concrete cure for at least two days.

Step B: Frame the Walls

1. Snap chalk lines on the slab for the wall plates.

2. Cut the 2 × 4 wall plates—use pressure-treated lumber for all bottom wall plates. Cut two bottom and two top plates at 137" for the side walls, and cut two bottom and two top plates at 144" for the front and rear walls.

3. Mark the stud layouts onto the plates following the FLOOR PLAN, on page 63.

4. Cut thirty-eight studs at 92⅝". Cut two jack studs at 78½" for the garage door opening and two at 75⅝" for the window opening.

5. Build two headers with 2 × 8s and ½" plywood: one at 99" for the garage door opening and one at 63" for the window.

6. Assemble, raise, and brace the walls one at a time. Use galvanized nails for attaching the studs to the bottom plates. When framing the front wall, assemble the studs, plates and header, then square the frame before cutting and installing the two 2 × 4 angle braces, as shown in the FRONT FRAMING ELEVATION, on page 62. Add the double top plates after raising the walls.

Step C: Install the Attic Floor Joists

1. Cut ten 2 × 6 attic joists at 144". Check each joist for crowning, then cut off the top corner at each end with a 1½" long 45° cut (this prevents the corners from projecting beyond the rafters).

2. Draw the rafter layout and attic joist layout onto the side walls, following the FRAMING ELEVATIONS, on page 62. The outside face of each end joist should fall 3½" from the outer faces of the front and rear wall, respectively (this leaves room for the 2 × 4 gable wall framing).

3. Install the joists with their ends flush with the side walls, fastening each end to the wall plate with three 8d toenails (two nails on one side, one on the opposite side).

Step D: Frame the Attic Kneewalls

1. Cut four 2 × 4 top plates at 144" and two bottom plates at 137". Cut twenty 2 × 4 studs at 26⅝" and four end studs at 33⅝".

2. Lay out the plates so the studs fall over the floor joists. The bottom plates should be flush with the outer faces of the end floor joists; the top plates should be even with the outsides of the front and rear walls. Position the end studs at the ends of the top plates, with their bottom ends on top of the wall plates below.

A. *Set the J-bolts into the wet concrete slab so they are plumb and extend 2½" above the surface.*

B. *Frame, square, and brace the front wall, then install the angle braces at the corners of the garage door opening.*

C. *Install the joists perpendicular to the side walls. All but the two outer joists sit next to a rafter.*

3. Snap chalk lines for the bottom plates, 18⅛" in from the ends of the floor joists.

4. Frame and raise the kneewalls, fastening their bottom plates to the attic joists with 16d nails. Plumb the walls and install temporary braces.

5. Install ¾" plywood over the joists between the kneewalls. Run the sheets perpendicular to the

D. *Install the kneewalls perpendicular to the attic joists. The kneewall top plates extend past the bottom plates by 3½".*

E. *Fasten the soffit ledgers to the studs, then cut and install blocks that run horizontally from the rafters to the ledgers.*

joists, and keep the outside edges flush with the end joists. Drive 8d nails every 6" along the edges and every 12" in the field of the sheets.

Step E: Frame the Roof

1. Cut two 2 × 8 nailers at 144". Fasten the nailers to the outsides of the kneewalls so their top edges are 32⅝" above the tops of the attic joists and their ends are flush with the end of the kneewalls—use 16d nails (see ELEVATIONS, page 62). Mark the rafter layouts onto the top edges and outside faces of the nailers.

2. Cut the 2 × 6 ridge board at 168", angle-cutting the front end at 16°.

3. Draw the rafter layout onto the ridge. The outer common rafters should be 16" from the front and 8" from the rear end of the ridge, respectively.

4. Cut two UPPER pattern rafters following the RAFTER TEMPLATE, on page 63, and cut one LOWER pattern rafter. Test-fit the rafters, then cut the remaining common rafters of each type. Cut six additional upper rafters and eight lower rafters for the gable overhangs, following the GABLE OVER-HANG RAFTER DETAILS, on page 65.

5. Install the common rafters. Nail the upper rafters to the ridge and kneewalls with 16d nails. Toenail the lower rafters to the nailer with 16d nails. Nail the rafters to the wall plate, then reinforce the connection with metal anchors, using the recommended nails. Facenail the attic joists to the rafters with two 10d nails at each end.

6. Cut the four 2 × 4 collar ties at 34" and fasten them between pairs of upper rafters, as shown in the BUILDING SECTION, on page 63 and the FRAMING ELEVATIONS, on page 62.

7. At each end of the building, level over from the bottom ends of the outer rafters and mark the wall studs. Snap a chalk line through the marks. This line represents the bottom edge of the soffit ledger (see the EAVE DETAIL, on page 65).

8. Cut two 2 × 4 soffit ledgers at 160", and nail them to the wall studs with their bottom edges on the chalk lines and their ends overhanging the walls by 8"—use 16d nails.

9. Cut twenty-four 2 × 4 blocks to fit between the soffit ledger and the outside ends of the rafters, as shown in the EAVE DETAIL, on page 65. Toenail the blocks to the ledgers and facenail them to the rafters with 10d nails.

Step F: Build the Gable Overhangs

1. Cut 2 × 4 lookouts at 5" and nail them to the inner overhang rafters, using 16" on-center spacing.

Don't install lookouts for the angled section of the front gable in this step.

2. Facenail the inner overhang rafters to the outer common rafters with 10d nails.

3. Cut the two angled overhang rafters for the front gable, following the GABLE OVERHANG RAFTER DETAILS, on page 65. Cut and test-fit the rafters and adjust the angles as needed. Fasten the rafters to the ridge and lookouts with 16d nails. Cut and install additional lookouts to fit between the angled overhang rafters and the inner overhang rafters.

4. Install the remaining overhang rafters to complete the gable overhangs.

Step G: Frame the Gable Walls

1. Cut the gable wall top plates to reach from the ridge to the attic kneewalls. Install the plates with their outside edges flush with the outer common rafters.

2. Mark the layouts for the gable studs onto the top plates of the main walls, following the FRONT and REAR FRAMING ELEVATIONS, on page 62. Use a plumb bob or a level to transfer the layout marks to the top plates. Install the gable studs with 8d nails.

3. Build the door header for the front wall. Mark the top corners of the header to follow the slope of the gable top plates, then cut off the corners. Install the header.

Step H: Install the Front Siding, Fascia & Soffits

Note: The fascia along the eaves is plowed—it has grooves cut into the inside faces for receiving the soffit panels. The fascia along the gable ends is not plowed.

1. Install the plywood siding on the front and rear walls, starting at the corners. Hold the siding 1" below the top of the concrete slab, and fasten it to the wall framing with 8d galv. finish nails. At the gable ends, install Z-flashing along the top edge of siding, then continue the siding up to the rafters. Below the attic door opening, stop the siding about ¼" below the top wall plate, as shown in the ATTIC DOOR SILL DETAIL, on page 66. Don't nail the siding along the garage door header until the flashing is installed.

2. Mill a ⅜"-wide × ¼"-deep groove into the fascia for the eave sides and gable ends—about 36 linear ft. (see the EAVE DETAIL, on page 65). Use a router or a table saw with a dado-head blade. Locate the groove so its bottom edge is ⅞" above the bottom edge of the fascia.

3. Install the 1 × 4 subfascia along the eaves, using 8d box nails (see the EAVE DETAIL, on page 65). Hold the bottom edge flush with ends of the rafters and the ends flush with the outer faces of the outer-most rafters.

4. Install the plowed fascia along the eaves so the

F. *Install the angled overhang rafters at the front gable, then cut and install lookouts to support the overhang rafters.*

G. *Use a plumb bob to transfer the gable stud layout to the top plate (overhang framing shown cutaway for clarity).*

top of the groove is flush with the bottom edge of the subfascia—use 8d galv. finish nails.

5. Cut perpendicular fascia pieces at the eave ends (where they meet the gable overhangs). The inside ends of these pieces should line up with the 1 × 4 corner trim, when it is installed (see the FRONT and REAR ELEVATIONS, on page 64). Cut short return pieces to run from the perpendicular fascia back to the wall. Make miter joints at all of the corners. Do not install the end and return pieces until the soffit panels are in place.

6. Install the fascia along the gable ends, holding it ½" above the rafters so it will be flush with the top of the roof sheathing. Angle-cut the bottom ends to meet flush with the end pieces.

7. Cut the soffit panels to fit between the fascia and the wall framing, allowing for the grooves and gable-end returns. Install the soffit panels, fastening them to the rafters (and soffit ledgers) with 3d galv. box nails.

8. Install the end and return fascia pieces.

9. Using plowed fascia, cut a triangular piece (called a *pork chop*) to finish the intersection between the gable and eave soffits. Cut a piece of soffit to enclose the space between the pork chop and the walls. Install these pieces.

10. Cut holes in the soffits and install four 4 × 12" soffit vents, as shown in the EAVE DETAIL, on page 65. Locate the vents within the second rafter bay from each end, on both sides of the building.

Step I: Install the Sheathing & Roofing

1. Install the ½" plywood roof sheathing, starting at a lower corner—use 8d box nails.

2. Attach metal drip edge along the eaves, then apply 15# building paper over the sheathing. Add drip edge along the gable ends, over the paper.

3. Install the asphalt shingles, starting at the eave edges. If desired, install roof vents (see page 37).

Step J: Install the Side Siding, Trim & Garage Door

1. Install the plywood siding along the side walls, butting the top edges against the soffit panels.

2. Install the 1 × 4 horizontal trim to cover the Z-flashing on the rear wall, but do not attach the piece at the front wall in this step. Install the corner trim so the bottom ends are flush with the bottom edges of the siding.

3. Cut the two 2 × 6 rails that will support the garage door tracks (consult the manufacturer's instructions to determine the length). Fasten them at the sides of the rough opening with 16d nails (see the GARAGE DOOR TRIM DETAIL, on page 66).

4. Rip cedar 1 × 8s for the door frame to match the depth of the garage door rough opening. Install the pieces around the opening, mitering the ends at about 22½° at the corner joints.

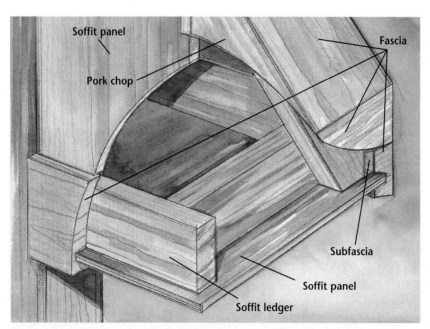

H. *Install the fascia and soffits at the eaves and gable overhangs. Add the return fascia pieces and a vertical soffit panel capped with a pork chop. (Drawing shown cutaway for clarity.)*

I. *Nail the sheathing every 6" along the edges and every 12" in the field.*

5. Cut the 1 × 4 trim to fit around the door frame, mitering the ends at the corner joints. Install flashing along the top of the door before installing the trim (see page 47). Install the trim.

6. Install the garage door, following the manufacturer's instructions.

Step K: Build the Window

1. Using ¾" × 4" stock, cut the window frame pieces to form a rectangular frame that is ½" shorter and narrower than the rough opening. Assemble the frame with 2½" deck screws.

2. Install the window frame in the rough opening, using shims. Make sure the frame is plumb and level and the jambs are straight, and fasten the frame with 10d galv. casing nails.

3. Cut eight 1 × 2 stops. Bevel the outer sill stop as shown in the WINDOW JAMB DETAIL, on page 66. Attach the inner stops with 6d galv. finish nails. Order the glass to fit.

4. Install the glass and outer stops, applying glazing tape to the stops on both sides of the glass.

5. Install the 1 × 4 window trim.

Step L: Build & Install the Attic Door

1. Rip cedar 1 × 6s to match the depth of the door rough opening. Cut the head jamb for the door frame at 59" and the side jambs at 39".

2. From full-width 1 × 6 stock, cut the sill at 57½". Cut a drip edge into the bottom face of the sill by making a ⅛"-deep saw cut about ¼" from front edge.

3. Fasten the head jamb to the ends of the side jambs with 2½" deck screws. Fasten the sill between the side jambs so it slopes down from back to front at 5° (see the ATTIC DOOR SILL DETAIL, on page 66). Install 1 × 2 stops at the sides and top of the frame, ¾" in from the front edges.

4. Install the frame in the rough opening, using shims or cedar shingles set on the bottom of the rough opening to support the sill along its length (this will prevent it from warping or splitting underfoot). Install the frame with shims and 10d galv. casing nails. The front edges of the side and top frame pieces should be flush with the face of the siding.

5. Build the storage doors following the ATTIC DOOR ELEVATION, on page 66. The outer dimensions of each door should be 28⅝" × 38". Cut the 1 × 8 panel boards about ⅛" short along the bottom to compensate for the slope of the sill (see the ATTIC DOOR SILL DETAIL). Fit the panel boards together, and trim the side pieces, if necessary. Fasten the boards to the 1 × 4 frame pieces with wood glue and 1¼" screws. Install the doors.

6. Install the horizontal 1 × 4 trim piece across the front wall, butting its top edge against the sill. Add trim around the top and sides of the door frame, butting the bottom ends of the sides on top of the horizontal trim.

J. *Frame the garage door rough opening with 1 × 8s ripped to fit.*

K. *Apply glazing tape to the inside window stops, then add the glass.*

L. *Set the attic door frame on shims to support the frame's sloped sill.*

Timber-frame Garden Shed

Timber-framing is a traditional building method that uses a simple framework of heavy timber posts and beams connected with hand-carved joints. From the outside, a timber-frame building looks like a standard, stick-framed structure, but the stout, rough-sawn members give the interior the feel of an 18th-century barn or workshop.

This 8 × 10-ft. shed has the same rough-sawn timbers and basic design used in traditional timber-framing, but with joints that are easy to make. In addition to an attractive interior, the shed

has a homemade skylight and a large side window that make it a bright, inviting space. If staying cool is a concern, install operable windows, or adapt the shed frame to add more windows. Adding roof vents can improve ventilation, as well.

The roof frame in this project is made with standard 2 × 4s, but if you're willing to pay a little more to improve the appearance, you can use rough-cut 2 × 4s or 4 × 4s for the roof framing.

Materials

Description	Quantity/Size	Material
Foundation		
Drainage material	25 cu. ft.	Compactible gravel
Skids	3 @ 10'-0"	4 × 4 treated timbers
Floor Framing		
Rim joists	2 @ 10'-0"	2 × 6 pressure-treated
Joists	9 @ 8'-0"	2 × 6 pressure-treated
Joist clip angles	18	3 × 3 × 3" × 18-gauge galvanized
Floor sheathing	3 sheets 4 × 8'	¾" tongue-&-groove ext.-grade plywood
Wall Framing		
Posts	6 @ 8'-0"	4 × 4 rough-sawn cedar
Window posts	2 @ 4'-0"	4 × 4 rough-sawn cedar
Girts	2 @ 10'-0", 2 @ 8'-0"	4 × 4 rough-sawn cedar
Beams	2 @ 10'-0", 2 @ 8'-0"	4 × 6 rough-sawn cedar
Braces	8 @ 2'-0"	4 × 4 rough-sawn cedar
Post bases	6, with nails	Simpson BC40
Post-beam connectors	8 pieces, with nails	Simpson LCE
L-connectors	4, with nails	Simpson A34
Roof Framing		
Rafters	12 @ 7'-0"	2 × 4
Collar ties	1 @ 10'-0"	2 × 4
Ridge board	1 @ 10'-0"	2 × 6
Metal anchors—rafters	8, with nails	Simpson H1
Gable-end blocking	4 @ 7'-0"	2 × 2
Exterior Finishes		
Siding	2 @ 14'-0", 8 @ 12'-0" 10 @ 10'-0", 29 @ 9'-0"	1 × 8 T&G V-joint rough-sawn cedar
Corner trim	8 @ 9'-0"	1 × 4 rough-sawn cedar
Fascia	4 @ 7'-0", 2 @ 12'-0"	1 × 6 rough-sawn cedar
Fascia trim	4 @ 7'-0", 2 @ 12'-0"	1 × 2 rough-sawn cedar
Subfascia	2 @ 12'-0"	1 × 4 pine
Plywood soffits	1 sheet 4 × 8'	⅜" cedar or fir plywood
Soffit vents	4 @ 4 × 12"	Louver with bug screen
Flashing (door)	4 linear ft.	Galvanized—18 gauge
Roofing		
Roof sheathing	6 sheets 4 × 8'	½" ext.-grade plywood
Asphalt shingles	1.7 squares	250# per square (min.)
15# building paper	140 sq. ft.	
Metal drip edge	2 @ 12'-0", 4 @ 7'-0"	Galvanized metal
Roof vents (optional)	2 units	
Roofing cement	1 tube	

Description	Quantity/Size	Material
Skylight		
Frame	1 @ 12'-0"	2 × 8
Glazing tape	24 linear ft.	
Stops	1 @ 12'-0"	1 × 2 clear redwood
Glass	1 piece—field measure	³⁄₁₆" tempered, clear (Optional: ¼" plexiglass, clear)
Flashing	14 linear ft.	Prefinished metal—24 gauge
Window		
Frame	4 @ 6'-0"	¾ x 4¼" (actual) S4S cedar
Mullion	1 @ 4'-0"	2 × 4 S4S cedar
Stops	8 @ 6'-0"	1 × 2 S4S cedar
Glazing tape	44 linear ft.	Glazing tape
Glass	2 pieces—field measure	¼" tempered, clear
Trim	4 @ 6'-0", 4 @ 4'-0"	1 × 3 rough-sawn cedar
Door		
Frame	2 @ 7'-0", 1 @ 4'-0"	¾ x 4¼" (actual) S4S cedar
Stops	2 @ 7'-0", 1 @ 4'-0"	1 × 2 S4S cedar
Panel material	7 @ 7'-0"	1 × 6 T&G V-joint rough-sawn cedar
Z-brace	2 @ 6'-0", 1 @ 8'-0"	1 × 6 rough-sawn cedar
Strap hinges	3	
Trim	5 @ 7'-0"	1 × 3 rough-sawn cedar
Fasteners		
60d common nails	16 nails	
20d common nails	32 nails	
16d galvanized common nails	3½ lbs.	
10d common nails	1 lb.	
10d galvanized casing nails	½ lb.	
8d galvanized box nails	1½ lbs.	
8d galvanized finish nails	7 lbs.	
8d box nails	¼ lb.	
6d galvanized finish nails	40 nails	
3d galvanized finish nails	50 nails	
1½" joist hanger nails	72 nails	
2½" deck screws	25 screws	
1¼" wood screws	50 screws	
⅞" galvanized roofing nails	2 lbs.	
⅜" × 6" lag screws	16 screws	
Silicone-latex caulk	2 tubes	
Construction adhesive	4 tubes	

FRONT FRAMING ELEVATION

LEFT SIDE FRAMING ELEVATION

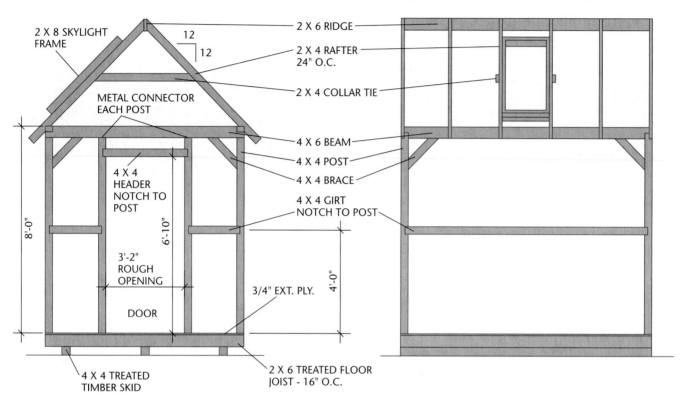

2 X 8 SKYLIGHT FRAME

12
12

METAL CONNECTOR EACH POST

4 X 4 HEADER NOTCH TO POST

8'-0"

6'-10"

3'-2" ROUGH OPENING

DOOR

4 X 4 TREATED TIMBER SKID

2 X 6 RIDGE

2 X 4 RAFTER 24" O.C.

2 X 4 COLLAR TIE

4 X 6 BEAM

4 X 4 POST

4 X 4 BRACE

4 X 4 GIRT NOTCH TO POST

3/4" EXT. PLY.

4'-0"

2 X 6 TREATED FLOOR JOIST - 16" O.C.

REAR FRAMING ELEVATION

RIGHT SIDE FRAMING ELEVATION

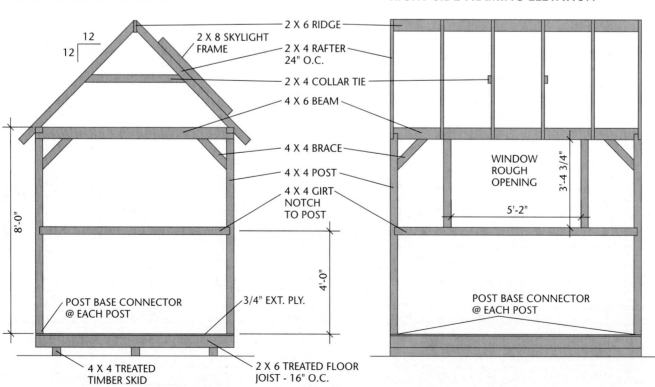

12
12

2 X 8 SKYLIGHT FRAME

2 X 6 RIDGE

2 X 4 RAFTER 24" O.C.

2 X 4 COLLAR TIE

4 X 6 BEAM

4 X 4 BRACE

4 X 4 POST

4 X 4 GIRT NOTCH TO POST

8'-0"

POST BASE CONNECTOR @ EACH POST

3/4" EXT. PLY.

4'-0"

4 X 4 TREATED TIMBER SKID

2 X 6 TREATED FLOOR JOIST - 16" O.C.

WINDOW ROUGH OPENING

3'-4 3/4"

5'-2"

POST BASE CONNECTOR @ EACH POST

BUILDING SECTION

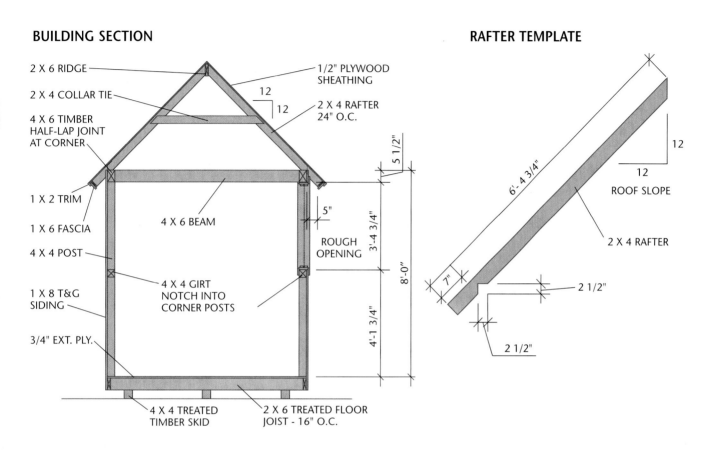

2 X 6 RIDGE

2 X 4 COLLAR TIE

4 X 6 TIMBER
HALF-LAP JOINT
AT CORNER

1 X 2 TRIM

1 X 6 FASCIA

4 X 4 POST

1 X 8 T&G
SIDING

3/4" EXT. PLY.

1/2" PLYWOOD
SHEATHING

12
12

2 X 4 RAFTER
24" O.C.

4 X 6 BEAM

5"

ROUGH
OPENING

5 1/2"

3'-4 3/4"

8'-0"

4'-1 3/4"

4 X 4 GIRT
NOTCH INTO
CORNER POSTS

4 X 4 TREATED
TIMBER SKID

2 X 6 TREATED FLOOR
JOIST - 16" O.C.

RAFTER TEMPLATE

6'- 4 3/4"

12
12

ROOF SLOPE

2 X 4 RAFTER

7"

2 1/2"

2 1/2"

FLOOR FRAMING PLAN

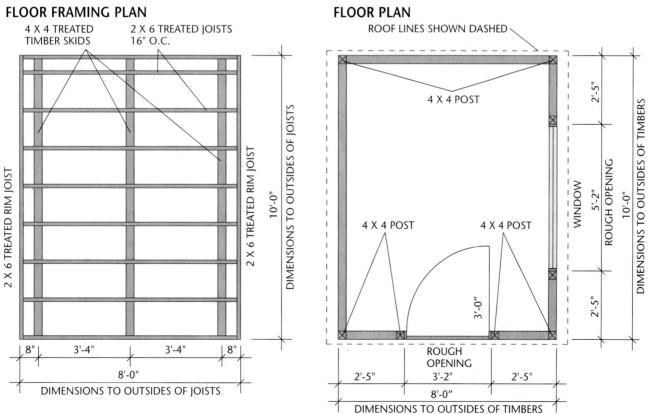

4 X 4 TREATED
TIMBER SKIDS

2 X 6 TREATED JOISTS
16" O.C.

2 X 6 TREATED RIM JOIST

2 X 6 TREATED RIM JOIST

10'-0"

DIMENSIONS TO OUTSIDES OF JOISTS

8"   3'-4"   3'-4"   8"

8'-0"

DIMENSIONS TO OUTSIDES OF JOISTS

FLOOR PLAN

ROOF LINES SHOWN DASHED

4 X 4 POST

4 X 4 POST

4 X 4 POST

WINDOW

ROUGH OPENING

2'-5"

5'-2"

2'-5"

10'-0"

DIMENSIONS TO OUTSIDES OF TIMBERS

3'-0"

ROUGH
OPENING

2'-5"   3'-2"   2'-5"

8'-0"

DIMENSIONS TO OUTSIDES OF TIMBERS

FRONT ELEVATION

LEFT SIDE ELEVATION

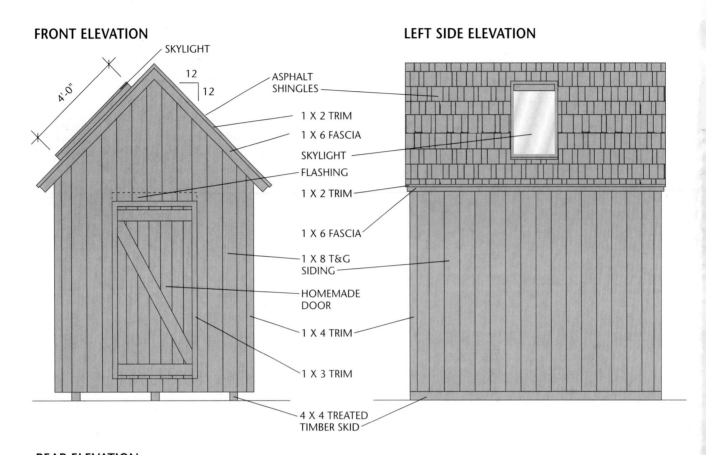

SKYLIGHT

4'-0"

12
12

ASPHALT
SHINGLES

1 X 2 TRIM

1 X 6 FASCIA

SKYLIGHT

FLASHING

1 X 2 TRIM

1 X 6 FASCIA

1 X 8 T&G
SIDING

HOMEMADE
DOOR

1 X 4 TRIM

1 X 3 TRIM

4 X 4 TREATED
TIMBER SKID

REAR ELEVATION

RIGHT SIDE ELEVATION

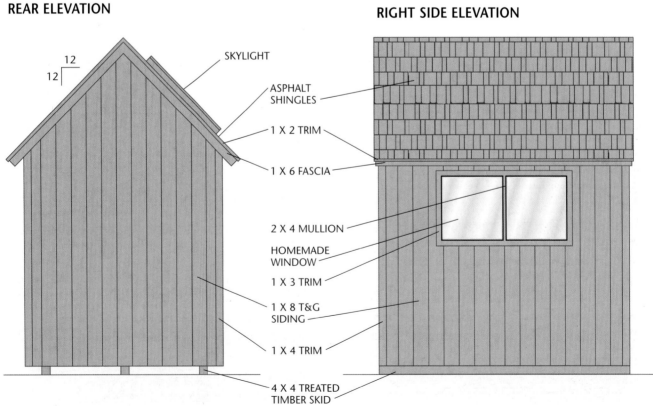

12
12

SKYLIGHT

ASPHALT
SHINGLES

1 X 2 TRIM

1 X 6 FASCIA

2 X 4 MULLION

HOMEMADE
WINDOW

1 X 3 TRIM

1 X 8 T&G
SIDING

1 X 4 TRIM

4 X 4 TREATED
TIMBER SKID

GABLE OVERHANG DETAIL

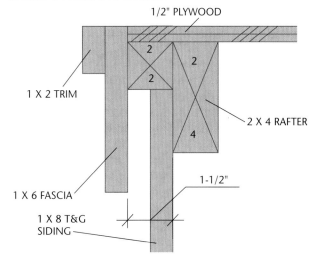

1/2" PLYWOOD

2

2

2

4

1 X 2 TRIM

2 X 4 RAFTER

1 X 6 FASCIA

1-1/2"

1 X 8 T&G
SIDING

EAVE DETAIL

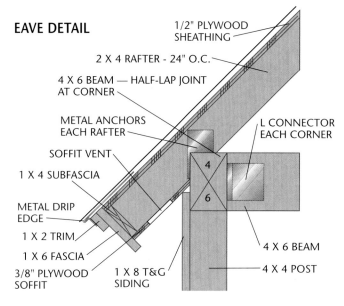

1/2" PLYWOOD
SHEATHING

2 X 4 RAFTER - 24" O.C.

4 X 6 BEAM — HALF-LAP JOINT
AT CORNER

METAL ANCHORS
EACH RAFTER

L CONNECTOR
EACH CORNER

SOFFIT VENT

4

6

1 X 4 SUBFASCIA

METAL DRIP
EDGE

1 X 2 TRIM

1 X 6 FASCIA

3/8" PLYWOOD
SOFFIT

1 X 8 T&G
SIDING

4 X 6 BEAM

4 X 4 POST

DOOR JAMB DETAIL

4 X 4 POST

1 X 3 TRIM

3/4" FRAME

4

4

3/4" BRD. DOOR
W/ 1 X 6 BRACE

1 X 2 STOP

1 X 8 T&G
SIDING

1 X 3 TRIM

1/4"

WINDOW JAMB DETAIL

1 X 8 T&G SIDING

1 X 3 TRIM

1 X 2 STOP

GLAZING TAPE
BOTH SIDES

4 X 4 POST

4

4

SLOPED STOP @ SILL

1/4" CLEAR GLASS
TEMPERED

1 X 2 STOP

1 X 3 TRIM

1/4"

3/4"

CUT SLOPE FOR
DRAINAGE

1/4"

1 X 2 CEDAR STOP
AT WINDOW SILL

SKYLIGHT DETAIL

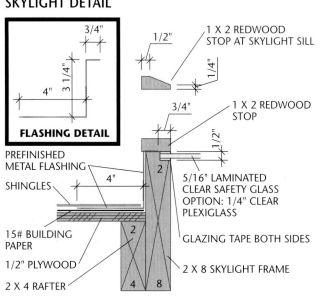

3/4"

3 1/4"

4"

FLASHING DETAIL

1/2"

1/4"

1 X 2 REDWOOD
STOP AT SKYLIGHT SILL

3/4"

1/2"

1 X 2 REDWOOD
STOP

2

PREFINISHED
METAL FLASHING

4"

SHINGLES

15# BUILDING
PAPER

2

4

8

1/2" PLYWOOD

2 X 4 RAFTER

5/16" LAMINATED
CLEAR SAFETY GLASS
OPTION: 1/4" CLEAR
PLEXIGLASS

GLAZING TAPE BOTH SIDES

2 X 8 SKYLIGHT FRAME

DOOR DETAIL

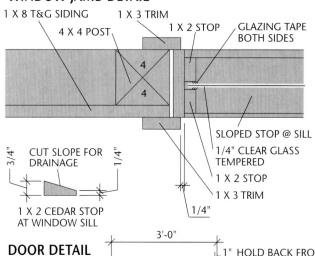

3'-0"

1" HOLD BACK FROM
DOOR EDGE

STRAP HINGE

1 X 8 BOARDS
GLUED AND
SCREWED TO
1 X 6 BOARDS

6'-8 3/4"

1 X 6 T&G
V-JT. BOARDS
VERTICAL

BUILDING THE TIMBER-FRAME GARDEN SHED

Step A: Build the Foundation & Floor Frame

1. Excavate the building site and add a 4" layer of compactible gravel. Tamp the gravel thoroughly, making sure it is level.

2. Cut three 4 × 4 treated timber skids at 120". Arrange and level the skids on the gravel bed, following the FLOOR FRAMING PLAN, on page 75.

3. Cut two 2 × 6 rim joists at 120" and nine joists at 93". Mark the joist layout onto the rim joists, following the plan. Assemble the frame with 16d galv. common nails—be sure to check each joist for crowning and install it with the crowned edge up.

4. Set the floor frame on top of the skids and measure the diagonals to make sure it's square. Install joist clip angles at each joist along the two outer skids, using 1½" joist hanger nails. Toenail each joist to the center skid with 16d galv. nails.

5. Install the tongue-and-groove floor sheathing, starting with a full sheet at one corner of the frame. Use 8d galv. box nails driven every 6" along the edges and every 12" in the field.

Step B: Cut & Notch the Posts

1. Cut six 4 × 4 posts at 90½", making sure both ends are square.

2. The four corner posts have 3½"-long × 1½"-deep notches on two adjacent sides, to accept the girts (note that the notches overlap each other by 1½"). Mark the bottoms of the notches at 46¼" from the bottom ends of the posts. Use a square to mark the complete outline of the notches.

The two door-frame posts each have one notch for a girt and one for the door header, also 3½"-long × 1½"-deep. Mark the bottom of the girt notches at 46¼" and the bottom of the header notches at 82".

3. Set a circular saw to cut exactly 1½" deep. Cut the notches one at a time: first make the cuts at the top and bottom of the notch, then make a series of cuts to remove the material in between. Clean out the notch with a sharp chisel. Test-fit the notch using the end of a 4 × 4—it should fit snugly.

4. Cut and test-fit the remaining notches.

Step C: Install the Posts

1. Position the post bases using a scrap piece of post. Fasten the bases to the floor with 16d galv. common nails, making sure the post sides are flush with the outside edges of the floor.

2. Install the door-post bases so the inside faces of the posts are 29" from the floor sides.

3. Set each post in its base, hold it plumb, and tack in one 16d galv. nail. Nail temporary cross-braces to the post. Use a level to set the post perfectly plumb, secure the braces, then fasten the post to the base with the recommended nails.

Step D: Cut & Install the Beams & Braces

1. Cut two 4 × 6 beams at 120" and two at 96", using a circular saw and handsaw or a power miter saw.

2. Cut the notches for the half-lap joints at the beam ends. Measure the width (4" nominal) and depth (6" nominal) of the beams, and mark the notches to equal the width × ½ of the depth. Orient the notches as shown in the FRAMING ELEVATIONS, on page

A. *Secure the floor frame to the foundation skids with angles (outside skids) and toenails (center skid).*

B. *Start the notches with a series of saw cuts, then remove the material with a sharp wood chisel.*

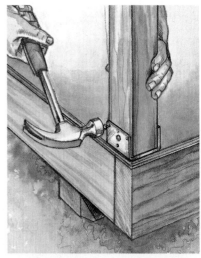

C. *Anchor the six posts to the floor with metal post bases. Use galvanized nails to fasten the bases and posts.*

74. Start the cuts with a circular saw, complete them with a handsaw, and smooth the notches with a chisel. Assemble the beams on the ground to test-fit the notches.

3. Set a 96" beam onto the front-wall posts and tack it in place with one 16d nail at each end. Measure the diagonals of the wall frame to make sure it's square. Drill pilot holes and drive two 60d common nails through each notch and into the post. Install the other 96" beam on the rear posts.

4. Set the 120" beams on top of the short beams, and check the side walls for squareness. Secure each half-lap joint with two 60d nails. Install a post-beam connector on the outside of each corner and on both sides of the door posts, using the recommended nails. Install an L-connector on the inside of each corner (see the EAVE DETAIL, on page 77), using the recommended nails.

5. Cut eight 4 × 4 corner braces at 20", mitering the ends at 45°. Position each brace at a corner so the ends are flush with the sides of the post and beam, and secure it with a bar clamp.

6. Drill a counterbored pilot hole 4½" from each end of the braces and fasten them to the beams and posts with ⅜" × 6" lag screws.

Step E: Install the Girts

1. Cut the 4 × 4 girts to fit between the posts.

2. To allow the girts to meet at the corner posts, notch both ends of the rear-wall girt and the outside end of each of the front-wall girts. Use a circular saw to cut the notches 1½"-wide × 1½" deep.

3. Test-fit the girts in the post notches. Apply construction adhesive to the notches and install the girts. Drill pilot holes and endnail the girts with two 20d nails driven through the outsides of the posts.

4. Cut and install the 4 × 4 door header in the same fashion. Cut the posts for the window rough opening. Position them following the FLOOR PLAN, on page 75, and fasten them with 20d toenails.

Step F: Frame the Roof

1. Cut two pattern rafters, following the RAFTER TEMPLATE, on page 75. Test-fit the rafters using a 2 × 6 spacer block to represent the ridge, then cut the ten remaining rafters.

2. Cut the 2 × 6 ridge board at 120". Draw the rafter layout onto the beams and ridge board, using 24" on-center spacing.

3. Install the rafters. Reinforce the rafter-beam connections with metal anchors on all but the four outer rafters, using the recommended nails.

4. Cut two 2 × 4 collar ties at 58", mitering the ends at 45°. Position the ties on the outside faces of the two middle rafters so they are level and their ends are ½" away from the tops of the rafters. Facenail them to the rafters with three 10d common nails at each end.

5. Cut four 2 × 2s to extend from the roof peak to the rafter ends (see the GABLE OVERHANG DETAIL, on page 77). Nail the 2 × 2s to the rafters with the top edges flush, using 10d nails.

6. Build the skylight frame, starting with the header and sill blocks. Measure from the ends of

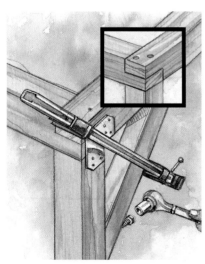

D. *Join the beams with half-lap joints (inset). Fasten the braces to the posts and beams with lag screws.*

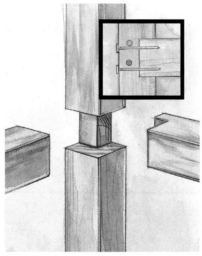

E. *Notch one girt end for each corner joint. Secure the girts to the posts with adhesive and 20d nails (inset).*

F. *Install blocks between the two middle rafters, then build the skylight frame from notched 2 × 8s.*

the two middle rafters and mark their inside faces at 16" and 64". Cut two 2 × 4 blocks to fit between the rafters at these marks. Set the blocks with their inside faces on the marks and their edges flush with the rafters, and endnail them with two 16d nails at each end (the blocks should be 48" apart).

7. Using a router or a table saw, cut a ¾"-wide × ½"-deep continuous notch into the top, corner edge of the skylight frame stock (see the SKYLIGHT DETAIL, on page 77.). Cut the frame pieces to length, mitering the ends at 45°. Position the frame pieces flush with the bottom edges of the rafters and facenail them with 10d nails.

8. Measure the frame at the notches and order the skylight glass to fit. Also order the metal flashing for the skylight frame.

Step G: Install the Siding on the Gable Ends

1. Install the 1 × 8 tongue-and-groove siding on the gable ends, starting at the corners. Hold the siding ¾" below the bottom of the floor frame and extend it up to the 2 × 2 blocking on the end rafters. Fasten the siding with 8d galvanized finish nails. Cut the boards flush to the insides of the door frame, but do not nail the siding to the door header in this step.

Step H: Install the Fascia, Soffits & Remaining Siding

1. Cut and install the 1 × 4 subfascia along the eaves (see the EAVE DETAIL, on page 77), using 8d box nails. Keep the ends flush with the outsides of the end rafters, and the top edges flush with the top rafter edges.

2. Install the 1 × 6 fascia and 1 × 2 trim along the gable overhangs, then along the eaves, using 8d galv. finish nails. Hold the fascia ½" above the rafters so it will be flush with the sheathing.

3. Rip the ⅜" plywood soffit panels to fit between the wall framing and the fascia (see the EAVE DETAIL, on page 77). Fasten the soffits to the rafters with 3d galv. box nails.

4. Cut holes for four soffit vents: locate one vent in each of the two outer rafter bays, on both sides of the building. Install the vents.

5. Install the siding along the side walls. Do not nail the siding to the window header in this step.

Step I: Install the Roofing

1. Install the ½" plywood sheathing, starting at a lower corner of the roof—use 8d box nails driven every 6" along the edges and every 12" in the field of the sheets.

2. Attach drip edge along the eaves, then apply 15# building paper over the sheathing. Add drip edge along the gable ends, on top of the paper.

3. Install the asphalt shingles up to the bottom edge of the skylight frame.

4. Add the pre-formed flashing around the skylight frame. Cut the bottom piece 8" longer than the width of the frame. Snip the horizontal flanges and bend the ends so they lie flat against the frame sides (the bottom piece goes on top of the

G. *Add the siding to the end walls, fastening it to the rafters and timber framing with two facenails at each support.*

H. *Install the subfascia along the eaves, then add the fascia and 1 × 2 trim along the top fascia edges.*

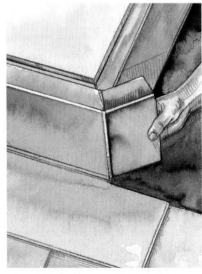

I. *Cut the horizontal flanges of the bottom piece of skylight flashing and wrap the ends around the frame sides.*

shingles). At each end, drive one roofing nail through the vertical flange into the frame side. Repeat this process to install the side flashing pieces, then the top piece. Seal all of the joints and nail heads with roofing cement.

5. Install the remaining shingles. If desired, install roof vents (see page 37.)

Step J: Complete the Skylight

1. Apply glazing tape to the notches of the sky-light frame. Set the glass over the tape, then apply tape along the glass edges (see the SKYLIGHT DETAIL, on page 77).

2. Using a table saw, circular saw, or hand plane, taper one side of a 26"-long piece of 1×2 stop material, as shown in the SKYLIGHT DETAIL.

3. Cut the stops to fit around the frame, using the tapered stop for the bottom (sill) piece. Drill pilot holes and attach the stops with 6d galv. finish nails.

4. Caulk the nail holes and along the stop edges.

Step K: Build & Install the Window

1. Using $\frac{3}{4}" \times 4\frac{1}{4}"$ stock, cut the window frame pieces to form a rectangular frame that is $\frac{1}{2}"$ shorter and narrower than the rough opening. Assemble the frame with $2\frac{1}{2}"$ deck screws. Cut and install a 2×4 mullion in the center of the frame (see page 59).

2. Install the window frame in the rough opening, using shims and a level to make sure the frame is plumb and level and the jambs are straight. Fasten the frame with 10d galv. casing nails.

3. Cut sixteen 1×2 stops. Bevel the two outer sill stops as shown in the WINDOW JAMB DETAIL, on page 77. Attach the inner stops with 6d galv. finish nails. Order the glass to fit.

4. Install the glass and outer stops, applying glazing tape to the stops on both sides of the glass.

Step L: Build the Door & Install the Trim

1. Cut the head jamb for the door frame at $37\frac{5}{8}"$ and the two side jambs at $80\frac{7}{8}"$. Position the head jamb over the ends of the side jambs and fasten the pieces with $2\frac{1}{2}"$ deck screws. Cut the 1×2 stops and install them $\frac{3}{4}"$ from the inside edges of the frame (see the DOOR JAMB DETAIL, on page 77). If you want the door to swing out, install the stops $\frac{3}{4}"$ from the outside edges.

2. Install the frame in the rough opening, using shims and 10d galv. casing nails. Make sure the frame is square and plumb.

3. Cut seven pieces of 1×6 siding at $80\frac{3}{4}"$. Fit the boards together with their ends flush, then mark the two end boards for trimming so that the total width is 36". Trim the end boards.

4. Cut the Z-brace boards following the DOOR DETAIL, on page 77. Lay the door on a flat surface and attach the brace boards using construction adhesive and $1\frac{1}{4}"$ wood screws. Install the bottom hinge before the cross brace. Install the remaining hinges and hang the door.

5. Install flashing above the door, nail off the siding, then install the 1×3 door trim. Install the 1×3 window trim and the 1×4 corner trim.

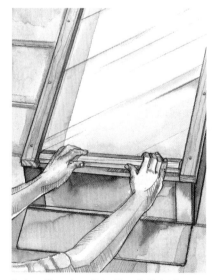

J. Lay the glass into the skylight frame and secure it with redwood stops. Use a beveled stop for the bottom piece.

K. Attach the outer window stops, with the beveled stop at the bottom. Nail the center stops to the mullion.

L. Use shims to set the gaps along the door edges, and mount the door hinges with galvanized screws.

Victorian Gazebo

A backyard gazebo provides open-air shelter from a hot sun or summer showers and is by itself a decorative landscape centerpiece. The classic octagonal gazebo in this project measures 9 feet across and has a cedar-decked floor perched about two feet above the ground. Its eight posts and floor deck are supported by poured concrete piers—your local building

department will tell you how deep to make them.

To improve the look of the gazebo on the inside, the roof is framed with cedar lumber instead of pine or fir. The roof sheathing is made up of 1×6 tongue-and-groove cedar boards and creates an attractive paneled ceiling.

By the nature of its shape, constructing a gazebo involves many angled cuts—for these, it will help you enormously to buy or rent a compound miter saw, or better yet, a sliding compound miter saw, which will cut angles on larger pieces of lumber.

Materials

Description	Quantity/Size	Material
Foundation		
Concrete	field measure	3,000 PSI concrete
Concrete tube forms	1 @ 16"-dia., 8 @ 12"-dia.	
Compactable gravel	2.5 cu. ft.	
Framing		
Posts	8 @ 10'-0"	6 × 6 cedar
Perimeter beams	8 @ 8'-0"	2 × 6 pressure-treated
Double joists	8 @ 10'-0"	2 × 6 pressure-treated
Angled joists	8 @ 8'-0"	2 × 6 pressure-treated
Roof beams	4 @ 10'-0"	6 × 8 cedar
Hip rafters	8 @ 8'-0"	2 × 6 cedar
Intermediate rafters	4 @ 10'-0"	2 × 6 cedar
Purlins	2 @ 8'-0"	2 × 6 cedar
Collar ties	4 @ 10'-0"	2 × 6 cedar
Rafter hub	1 @ 2'-0"	8 × 8 cedar
Wood sphere	1 @ 10"-dia., with dowel screw	
Pad (center pier)	Cut from stringers	2 × 12 pressure-treated
Framing anchors		
Perimeter beams to posts	8, with nails	Simpson U26-2
Angled joists to perim. beams	16, with nails	Simpson U26
Angled joists to double joists	16, with nails	Simpson LSU26
Anchor bolts	9 @ ⅝" × 12"	Galvanized J-bolt
Posts to piers	8, with fasteners	Simpson ABU66
Perimeter beams to posts	32	½" × 6" lag screws & washers
Metal anchors—rafters to beams	24	Simpson H1
Metal anchors—rafters to hub	8, with nails	Simpson FB26
Posts to beams	8, with fasteners	Simpson 1212T
Beams to beams	8, with nails	3" × 12" × 14-gauge galv. plate
Stringers to perimeter beam	8, with nails	Simpson L50
Stairs		
Compactible gravel	4.5 cu. ft.	
Concrete form	2 @ 8'-0"	2 × 4
Stair pad	7 @ 60-lb. bags	Concrete mix

Description	Quantity/Size	Material
Stairs (cont.)		
Stringers	3 @ 8'-0"	2 × 12 pressure-treated
Stair treads	2 @ 10'-0"	2 × 6 cedar
Stair risers	1 @ 10'-0"	1 × 8 cedar
Finishing Lumber		
Decking	15 @ 8'-0", 6 @ 10'-0"	2 × 6 cedar
Deck starter	1 @ 1'-0"	2 × 8 cedar
Fascia	4 @ 10'-0"	2 × 4 cedar
Lattice	4 panels @ 4 × 8'	Cedar lattice
Stops	15 @ 8'-0" (horizontal)	5/4 × 5/4 cedar
	10 @ 10'-0" (vertical)	
Rails	11 @ 8'-0"	2 × 4 cedar
Roofing		
Roof sheathing	26 @ 8'-0", 14 @ 10'-0"	1 × 6 T&G V-joint cedar
Asphalt shingles	256 sq. ft.	
15# building paper	300 sq. ft.	
Metal drip edge	36 linear ft.	
Galvanized flashing	3 linear ft.	
Roofing cement	1 tube	
Fasteners		
16d common nails	2½ lbs.	
16d galvanized common nails	1 lb.	
16d galvanized box nails	3 lbs.	
16d galvanized casing nails	1 lb.	
10d galvanized common nails	4½ lbs.	
8d galvanized box nails	3½ lbs.	
8d galvanized finish nails	2 lbs.	
3d galvanized finish nails	⅛ lb.	
1½" galvanized joist hanger nails	24 nails	
Masonry screws or nails	6 screws/nails	
3" deck screws	650 screws	
Construction adhesive	1 tube	

BUILDING SECTION

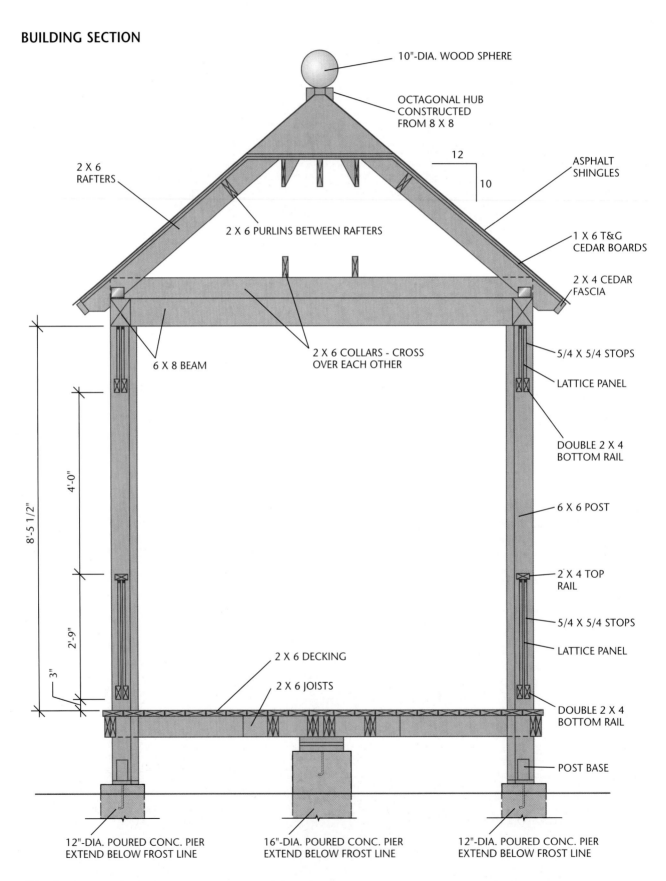

10"-DIA. WOOD SPHERE

OCTAGONAL HUB
CONSTRUCTED
FROM 8 X 8

12
10

2 X 6
RAFTERS

ASPHALT
SHINGLES

2 X 6 PURLINS BETWEEN RAFTERS

1 X 6 T&G
CEDAR BOARDS

2 X 4 CEDAR
FASCIA

2 X 6 COLLARS - CROSS
OVER EACH OTHER

6 X 8 BEAM

5/4 X 5/4 STOPS

LATTICE PANEL

DOUBLE 2 X 4
BOTTOM RAIL

6 X 6 POST

8'-5 1/2"

4'-0"

2'-9"

3"

2 X 4 TOP
RAIL

5/4 X 5/4 STOPS

LATTICE PANEL

2 X 6 DECKING

2 X 6 JOISTS

DOUBLE 2 X 4
BOTTOM RAIL

POST BASE

12"-DIA. POURED CONC. PIER
EXTEND BELOW FROST LINE

16"-DIA. POURED CONC. PIER
EXTEND BELOW FROST LINE

12"-DIA. POURED CONC. PIER
EXTEND BELOW FROST LINE

FRONT ELEVATION

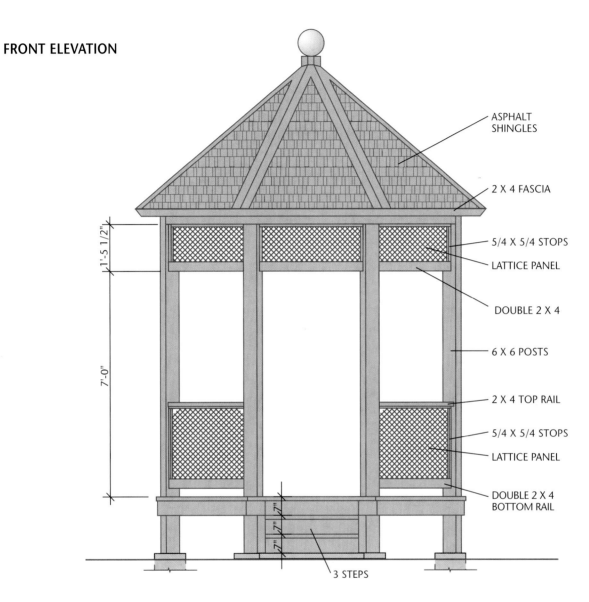

ASPHALT
SHINGLES

2 X 4 FASCIA

5/4 X 5/4 STOPS

LATTICE PANEL

DOUBLE 2 X 4

6 X 6 POSTS

2 X 4 TOP RAIL

5/4 X 5/4 STOPS

LATTICE PANEL

DOUBLE 2 X 4
BOTTOM RAIL

1'-5 1/2"

7'-0"

7"
7"
7"

3 STEPS

CENTER PIER DETAIL

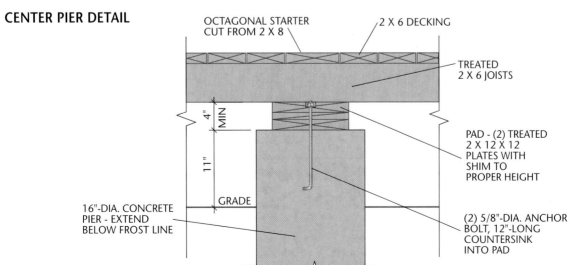

OCTAGONAL STARTER
CUT FROM 2 X 8

2 X 6 DECKING

TREATED
2 X 6 JOISTS

PAD - (2) TREATED
2 X 12 X 12
PLATES WITH
SHIM TO
PROPER HEIGHT

(2) 5/8"-DIA. ANCHOR
BOLT, 12"-LONG
COUNTERSINK
INTO PAD

16"-DIA. CONCRETE
PIER - EXTEND
BELOW FROST LINE

4" MIN

11"

GRADE

Projects

FLOOR FRAMING PLAN

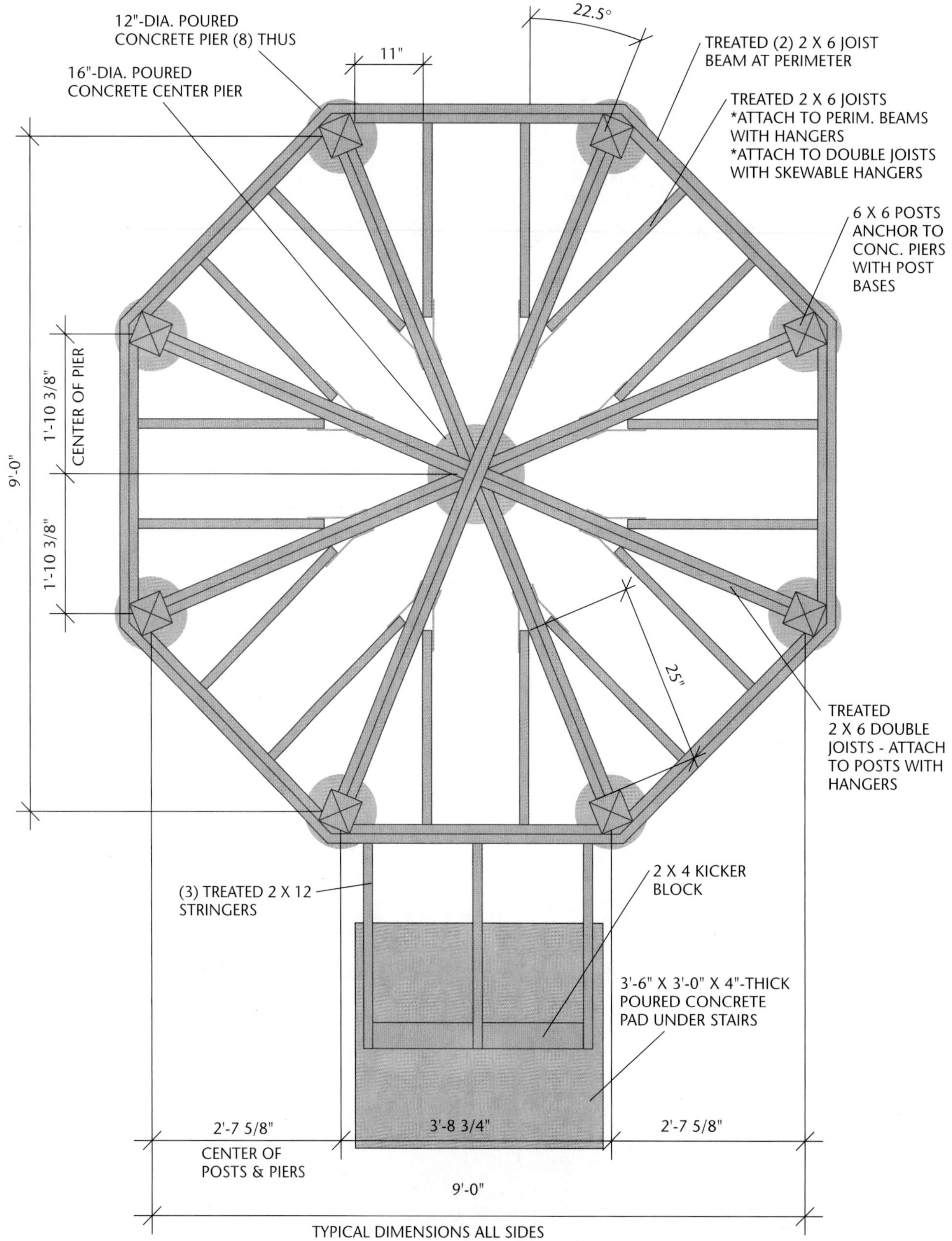

12"-DIA. POURED
CONCRETE PIER (8) THUS

16"-DIA. POURED
CONCRETE CENTER PIER

11"

22.5°

TREATED (2) 2 X 6 JOIST
BEAM AT PERIMETER

TREATED 2 X 6 JOISTS
*ATTACH TO PERIM. BEAMS
WITH HANGERS
*ATTACH TO DOUBLE JOISTS
WITH SKEWABLE HANGERS

6 X 6 POSTS
ANCHOR TO
CONC. PIERS
WITH POST
BASES

9'-0"

1'-10 3/8"   CENTER OF PIER

1'-10 3/8"

25"

TREATED
2 X 6 DOUBLE
JOISTS - ATTACH
TO POSTS WITH
HANGERS

(3) TREATED 2 X 12
STRINGERS

2 X 4 KICKER
BLOCK

3'-6" X 3'-0" X 4"-THICK
POURED CONCRETE
PAD UNDER STAIRS

2'-7 5/8"

3'-8 3/4"

2'-7 5/8"

CENTER OF
POSTS & PIERS

9'-0"

TYPICAL DIMENSIONS ALL SIDES

DECKING PLAN

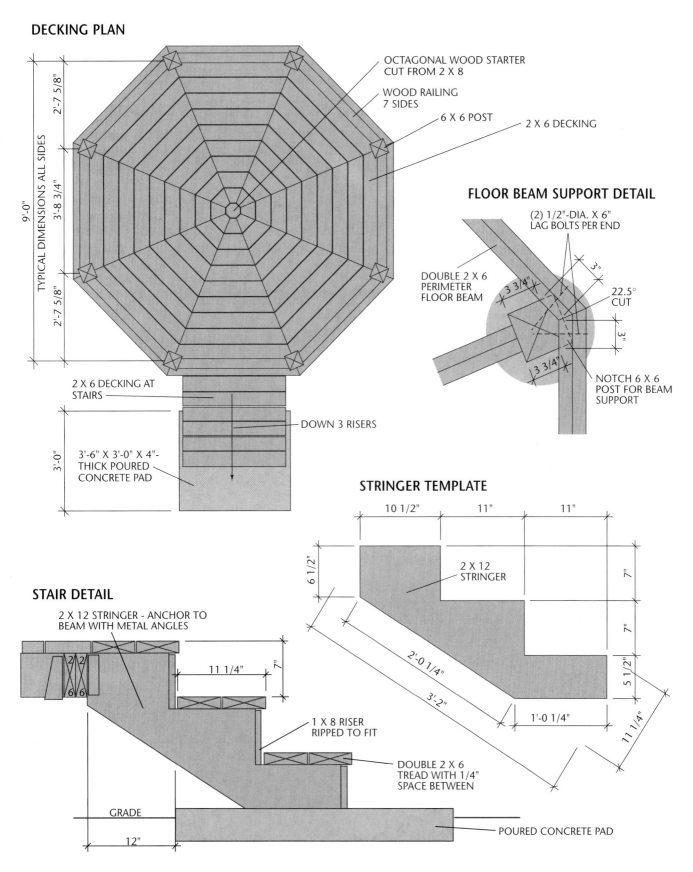

OCTAGONAL WOOD STARTER
CUT FROM 2 X 8

WOOD RAILING
7 SIDES

6 X 6 POST

2 X 6 DECKING

TYPICAL DIMENSIONS ALL SIDES

2'-7 5/8"

3'-8 3/4"

2'-7 5/8"

9'-0"

2 X 6 DECKING AT
STAIRS

DOWN 3 RISERS

3'-0"

3'-6" X 3'-0" X 4"-
THICK POURED
CONCRETE PAD

FLOOR BEAM SUPPORT DETAIL

(2) 1/2"-DIA. X 6"
LAG BOLTS PER END

DOUBLE 2 X 6
PERIMETER
FLOOR BEAM

3 3/4"

3"

22.5°
CUT

3"

3 3/4"

NOTCH 6 X 6
POST FOR BEAM
SUPPORT

STRINGER TEMPLATE

10 1/2"

11"

11"

6 1/2"

7"

7"

5 1/2"

2 X 12
STRINGER

2'-0 1/4"

3'-2"

1'-0 1/4"

11 1/4"

STAIR DETAIL

2 X 12 STRINGER - ANCHOR TO
BEAM WITH METAL ANGLES

2 2

6 6

11 1/4"

7"

1 X 8 RISER
RIPPED TO FIT

DOUBLE 2 X 6
TREAD WITH 1/4"
SPACE BETWEEN

GRADE

12"

POURED CONCRETE PAD

ROOF FRAMING PLAN

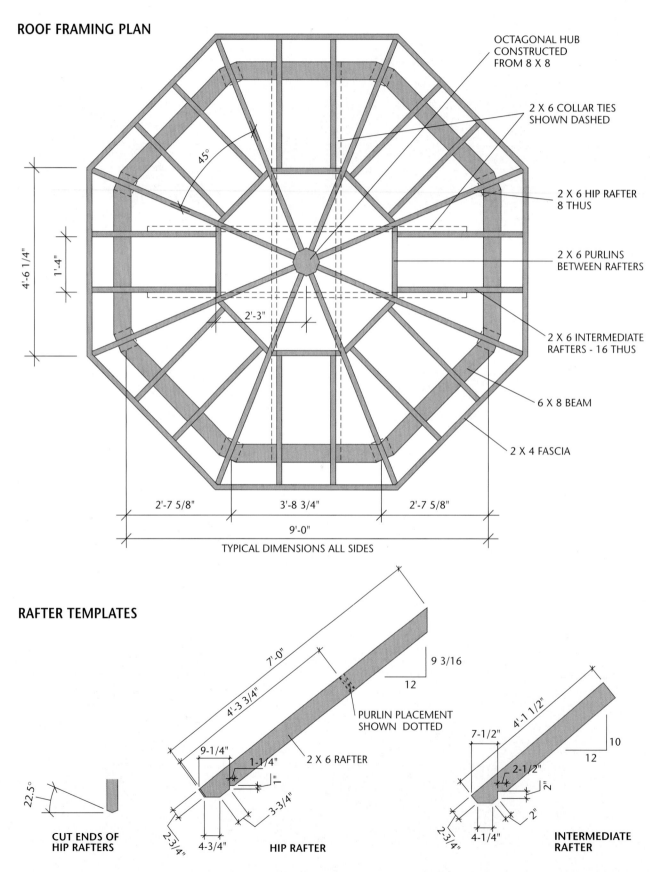

OCTAGONAL HUB
CONSTRUCTED
FROM 8 X 8

2 X 6 COLLAR TIES
SHOWN DASHED

2 X 6 HIP RAFTER
8 THUS

2 X 6 PURLINS
BETWEEN RAFTERS

2 X 6 INTERMEDIATE
RAFTERS - 16 THUS

6 X 8 BEAM

2 X 4 FASCIA

45°

4'-6 1/4"

1'-4"

2'-3"

2'-7 5/8"   3'-8 3/4"   2'-7 5/8"

9'-0"

TYPICAL DIMENSIONS ALL SIDES

RAFTER TEMPLATES

7'-0"

4'-3 3/4"

9 3/16
12

PURLIN PLACEMENT
SHOWN DOTTED

9-1/4"

1-1/4"

1"

2 X 6 RAFTER

3-3/4"

2-3/4"

4-3/4"

22.5°

**CUT ENDS OF
HIP RAFTERS**

HIP RAFTER

4'-1 1/2"

10
12

7-1/2"

2-1/2"

2"

2"

2-3/4"

4-1/4"

**INTERMEDIATE
RAFTER**

DETAIL AT DECK EDGE

2 X 4 CEDAR TOP RAIL

5/4 X 5/4 CEDAR STOPS BOTH SIDES

2'-9"

LATTICE PANEL

2 X 4 CEDAR BOTTOM RAIL BOTH SIDES

3"

2 X 6 DECKING

1/2"

(2) 2 X 6 TREATED JOIST BEAM

TREATED 2 X 6 JOISTS

POST BASE ANCHOR TO PIER

GRADE

5/8"-DIA. X 12" J-BOLT ANCHOR

12"-DIA. CONCRETE PIER EXTEND BELOW FROST LINE

ROOF EDGE DETAIL

ASPHALT SHINGLES

15# BUILDING PAPER

1 X 6 T&G V-JOINT CEDAR BOARDS

METAL DRIP EDGE

METAL ANCHORS @ EACH RAFTER

6 X 8 TIMBER BEAM

TEE STRAP ANCHOR POST TO BEAM

2 X 4 FASCIA

5/4 X 5/4 CEDAR STOPS BOTH SIDES

1'-5 1/2"

LATTICE PANEL

2 X 4 CEDAR BOTTOM RAIL BOTH SIDES

RAFTER HUB DETAIL

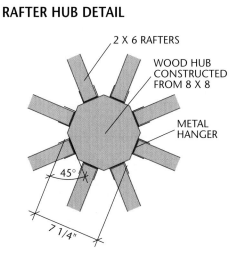

2 X 6 RAFTERS

WOOD HUB CONSTRUCTED FROM 8 X 8

METAL HANGER

45°

7 1/4"

CORNER DETAIL AT ROOF BEAM LINE

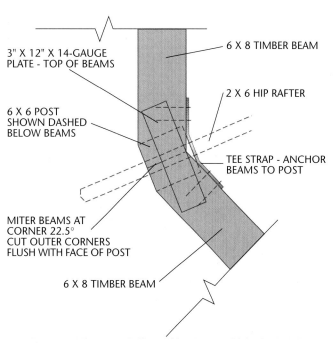

6 X 8 TIMBER BEAM

3" X 12" X 14-GAUGE PLATE - TOP OF BEAMS

2 X 6 HIP RAFTER

6 X 6 POST SHOWN DASHED BELOW BEAMS

TEE STRAP - ANCHOR BEAMS TO POST

MITER BEAMS AT CORNER 22.5° CUT OUTER CORNERS FLUSH WITH FACE OF POST

6 X 8 TIMBER BEAM

BUILDING THE VICTORIAN GAZEBO

Step A: Pour the Concrete Pier Footings

Note: See pages 14 to 17 for instructions on laying out and pouring concrete pier footings. Use 12"-dia. cardboard tube forms for the eight outer piers and a 16"-dia. form for the center pier.

1. Set up batter boards in a square pattern, and attach tight mason's lines to form a 9 × 9-ft. square. Take diagonal measurements to make sure the lines are square to one another. Attach two more lines that run diagonally from the corners and cross in the center of the square—this intersection represents the center of the center footing.

2. Measure 31⅝" in both directions from each corner and make a mark on a piece of tape attached to the line. These points represent the centers of the eight outer footings.

3. At each of the nine points, use a plumb bob to transfer the point to the ground, and mark the point with a stake. Remove the mason's lines.

4. Dig holes for the forms and add a 4" layer of gravel to each hole. Set the forms so the tops of the outer forms are 2" above grade and the center form is 11" above grade. Level the forms and secure them with packed soil. Restring the mason's lines and confirm that the forms are centered under the nine points.

5. Fill each form with concrete. Screed the tops, then insert a ⅝" × 12" J-bolt in the center of the form. Use a plumb bob to align the J-bolt with the point on the line layout. On the outer footings, set the bolts so they protrude ¾" to 1" from the concrete; on the center footing, set the bolt to protrude 5". Let the concrete cure completely.

Step B: Set the Posts

1. Use a straight board to mark reference lines for squaring the post anchors. Set the board on top of one of the outer footings and on the center footing. Holding the board against the same side of the J-bolts, draw a pencil line along the board across the tops of the footings. Do the same for the remaining footings.

2. Place a metal post anchor on each footing and center it over the J-bolt. Use a framing square to position the anchor so it's square to the reference line (see photo F, on page 17). Secure the anchor with washers and a nut.

3. Set each post in an anchor, tack it in place with a nail, then brace it with temporary cross braces so that it's perfectly plumb. Secure the post to the anchor, using the fasteners recommended by the manufacturer. (Note: You will cut the posts to length during the construction of the roof frame.)

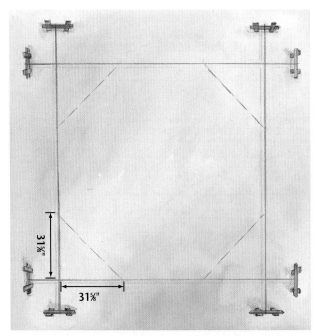

A. *Measure in 31⅝" from the corners of the string layout to mark the centers of the outside piers.*

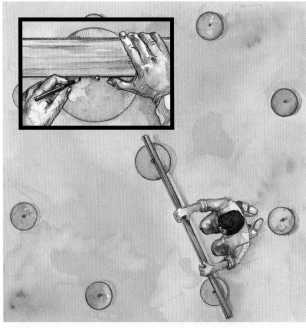

B. *Set a board across the center and each outer footing and mark a line across the top of the outer footing.*

Step C: Install the Perimeter Floor Beams

1. Starting at one of the posts that will be nearest to the stairs, measure from the ground and mark the post at 20½". Draw a level line at this mark around all four sides of the post. Transfer this height mark to the other posts, using a mason's line and a line level. These marks represent the tops of the 2 × 6 perimeter beams and the double joists of the floor frame.

2. Measure down 5½" from the post marks and make a second mark on all sides of each post. Notch the outer posts to accept the inner member of the perimeter floor beams, as shown in the FLOOR BEAM SUPPORT DETAIL, on page 87, using a handsaw or circular saw and a chisel.

3. Cut the inner members of the perimeter floor beams to extend between the centers of the notches of adjacent posts, angling the ends at 22½°. Set the members into the notches and tack them to the posts with two 16d galv. common nails.

4. Cut the outer members of the perimeter beams to fit around the inner members, angling the ends at 22½° so they fit together at tight miter joints (you may have to adjust the angles a little). Anchor the perimeter beams to the posts with two ½" × 6" lag screws at each end, as shown in the FLOOR BEAM SUPPORT DETAIL. Fasten the inner and outer beams together with pairs of 10d galv. common nails driven every 12".

Step D: Install the Double Joists

1. Fasten metal anchors to the centers of the posts so the tops of the joists will be flush with the upper line drawn in Step C (also, see the FLOOR FRAMING PLAN, on page 86).

2. Cut two 2 × 6 joists to span between two opposing posts, as shown in the FLOOR FRAMING PLAN (check the boards for crowning, and make sure to install them crown-up). Nail the joists together with pairs of 10d galv. common nails spaced every 12".

3. Set the double joist into the hangers and leave it in place while you build and fit the wood pad that supports the joists at the center pier (see the CENTER PIER DETAIL, on page 85).

4. Cut two 2 × 12 plates—one from two of the boards you'll use for the stair stringers—and cut a shim at 11¼". Use treated plywood or treated lumber for the shim (if necessary, sand a lumber shim to the correct thickness with a belt sander.) Test-fit the pad, then remove the joist.

5. Fasten together the plates and shim with 16d galv. nails. Drill a counterbore hole for the anchor nut and washer into the top plate, then drill a ⅝" hole through the center of the plates and shim.

C. Cut the post notches by making horizontal cuts with a handsaw then removing the material with a chisel.

D. Miter the ends of four of the double joists so they meet flush with the full-length joist and those perpendicular to it.

Secure the pad to the pier with construction adhesive and an anchor nut and washer.

6. Install the double joist, fastening it to the anchors with the recommended nails and toenailing it to the center pad with 10d galv. nails.

7. Cut and assemble two double joists that run perpendicular to the full-length double joist. Install the joists at the midpoint of the full-length joist, toenailing them to the joist and pad.

8. Cut the remaining four double joists so their inside ends taper together at 45°. Install the joists following the FLOOR FRAMING PLAN, on page 86.

Step E: Install the Angled Floor Joists

1. Mark the perimeter beam 11" from the post sides to represent the outside faces of the sixteen floor joists (see the FLOOR FRAMING PLAN, on page 86). Then, measure from the inside face of each post toward the center and mark both sides of the double joists at 25"—this mark represents the end of the angled joist.

2. Install metal joist anchors on the perimeter beams and skewable anchors on the double joists, using the recommended fasteners.

3. Cut and install the 2 × 6 angled floor joists, following the anchor manufacturer's instructions.

Step F: Pour the Stair Pad

Note: The concrete pad sits square to one side of the floor frame, 12" from the outside face of the perimeter beam (see the STAIR DETAIL, on page 87).

1. Using stakes or mason's line, mark a rectangular area that is 39 × 49", positioning its long side 10½" from the perimeter beam. Center the rectangle between the two nearest posts.

2. Excavate within the area to a depth of 7". Add 4" of compactible gravel and tamp it thoroughly.

3. Build a form from 2 × 4 lumber that is 36" × 42" (inner dimensions). Set the form with stakes so that the inside face of its long side is 12" from the perimeter beam and the form is centered between the nearest posts. Make sure the top of the form is level and is 19½" from the top of the perimeter beam.

4. Fill the form with concrete, screed the top flat, and float the concrete, if desired (see pages 20 to 21). Round over the edges of the pad with a concrete edger. Let the concrete cure for 24 hours, then remove the form and backfill around the pad with soil or gravel.

Step G: Build the Stairs

Note: The STRINGER TEMPLATE, on page 87, is designed for a gazebo that measures 21" from the stair pad to the top of the floor deck. If your gazebo is at a different height, adjust the riser dimension of the steps to match your project: divide the floor

E. *Fasten the angled floor joists to the sides of the double joists with skewable (adjustable) metal anchors.*

F. *Fill the 2 × 4 form for the stair pad with concrete, then screed the top with a straight piece of 2 × 4.*

height (including the decking) by three to find the riser height for each step.

1. Use a framing square to lay out the first 2×12 stair stringer, following the STRINGER TEMPLATE: Starting at one end of the board, position the framing square along the top edge of the board. Align the 11" mark on the square's blade (long part) and the 7" mark on the tongue (short part) with the edge of the board. Trace along the outer edges of the blade and tongue, then use the square to extend the blade marking to the other edge of the board. The tongue mark represents the first riser.

2. Measure 1½" from the bottom mark and draw another line that is parallel to it—this is the cutting line for the bottom of the stringer (the 1½" is an allowance for the thickness of the treads of the first step).

3. Continue the step layout, starting at the point where the first riser mark intersects the top edge of the board. Draw lines for the tread of the first step and the riser of the second step. Repeat this process to draw one more step and a top cutting line.

4. Measure 10½" from the top riser and make a mark on the top cutting line. Draw a perpendicular line from the cutting line to the opposite edge of the board—this line represents the top end cut.

5. Cut the stringer and test-fit it against the stair

pad and perimeter beam. Make any necessary adjustments. Using the stringer as a pattern, trace the layout onto the two remaining stringer boards, then cut the stringers.

6. Attach the stringers to the perimeter floor beam with metal angles, following the layout shown in the FLOOR FRAMING PLAN on page 86.

7. From scrap pressure-treated 2×4 lumber, cut kicker blocks to fit between the bottom ends of the stair stringers. Fasten the blocks to the concrete pad with construction adhesive and masonry screws or nails, then nail through the sides of the stringers into the kickers with 16d galv. common nails.

Step H: Install the Decking

1. Cut an octagonal starter piece from a cedar 2×8: Draw two lines across the board to make a $7\frac{1}{4} \times 7\frac{1}{4}$" square. Make a mark 2⅛" in from each corner, then connect the marks to form an octagon. Cut the starter piece and position it in the center of the floor frame, with each point centered on a double joist. Drill pilot holes and attach the piece with 3" deck screws.

2. Cut the 2×6 deck boards for each row one at a time. The end cuts for each boards should be 22½°, but you may have to adjust the angles occasionally to make tight joints. Gap the boards, if desired, but make sure the gaps are consistent—use scrap wood

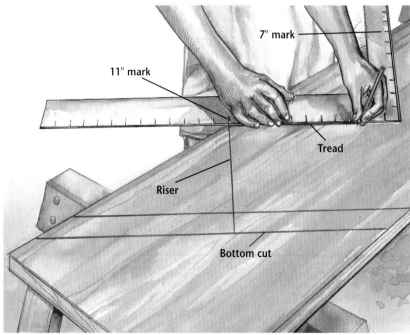

G. *Align the framing square with the top edge of the board. Make the 11" tread mark by tracing along the square's tongue, the riser mark along the blade.*

H. *Install the decking by completing one row at a time.*

or nails as spacers. Drill pilot holes and drive two screws wherever a board meets a framing member. Measure periodically to make sure the boards are parallel to the perimeter beams. Overhang the perimeter beams by ½" with the outer row of decking.

3. Install the 2 × 6 treads and 1 × 8 riser boards on the stairs following the STAIR DETAIL, on page 87.

Step I: Set the Roof Beams

1. Measure up from the floor deck and mark one of the posts at 101½". Transfer that mark to the remaining posts, using a mason's line and a line level. Mark a level cutting line around all sides of each post, then cut the posts with a reciprocating saw or handsaw.

2. On the top of each post, draw a line down the middle that points toward the center of the structure. Cut each of the four 6 × 8 timber beams in half so you have eight 5-ft.-long beams.

3. Set each beam on top of two neighboring posts so its outside face is flush with the outside corners of the posts. Mark the inside face of the beam where it meets the post centerlines—these marks represent cuts at each end (see the CORNER DETAIL AT ROOF BEAM LINE, on page 89). Also mark the underside of the beam by tracing along the outside faces of the posts—these lines show

you where to trim off the beams so they will be flush with the outside post faces. Use a square to extend the marks down around the post sides to help keep your cuts straight.

4. Starting from the end-cut marks, cut the beam ends at 22½°. Trim off the corners at the underside marks. Mark and cut the remaining beams, test-fitting the angles as you go.

5. Install the beams, securing them to the posts with metal T-anchors. Bend the side flanges of the anchors, as shown in the CORNER DETAIL AT ROOF BEAM LINE, on page 89, and fasten the anchors with the recommended fasteners. Tie the beams together with galvanized metal plates fastened with 16d galv. box nails.

Step J: Install the Hip Rafters

1. Cut the roof hub from an 8 × 8 post, following the RAFTER HUB DETAIL on page 89. You can have the hub cut for you at a lumberyard or cut it yourself using a table saw or circular saw. Cut the post at 16", then mark an octagon on each end: make a mark 2⅛" in from each corner, then join the marks. The cuts are at 45°. If you use a circular saw, extend the cutting lines down the sides of the post to ensure straight cuts.

2. Draw a line around the perimeter of the hub,

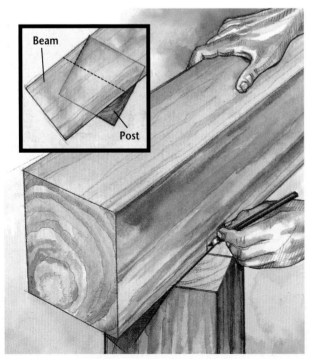

I. *Mark the inside faces of the beams at the post centerlines. Mark the beam undersides along the outside post faces.*

J. *Attach the rafters to the anchors on the roof hub, driving the nails at a slight angle, if necessary.*

3½" from the bottom end. Center a metal anchor on each hub side, with its bottom flush to the line, and fasten it to the hub using the recommended nails.

3. Cut two pattern 2 × 6 hip rafters, following the RAFTER TEMPLATES on page 88. Tack the rafters to opposing sides of the hub and test-fit the rafters on the roof beams. The bottom rafter ends should fall over the post centers. Make any necessary adjustments to the rafter cuts.

4. Use a pattern rafter to mark and cut the six remaining hip rafters. Install the rafters, toenailing the bottom ends to the roof beams with one 16d common nail on each side. Fasten the top ends to the anchors with 1½" galv. joist hanger nails, then install metal anchors at the bottom rafter ends, using the recommended nails.

Step K: Install Purlins & Intermediate Rafters

1. On each side of each hip rafter, measure up from the cut edge at the lower rafter end and make a mark at 51¾"—these marks represent the lower faces of the purlins (see the ROOF FRAMING PLAN, on page 88, the BUILDING SECTION, on page 84, and the RAFTER TEMPLATES, on page 88).

2. Cut the 2 × 6 purlins, beveling the ends at 22½°. Position them between the rafters so their top edges are flush with the top edges of the rafters.

Endnail or toenail the purlins to the rafters with 16d common nails.

3. Mark the layout for the intermediate rafters onto the tops of the roof beams, following the ROOF FRAMING PLAN, on page 88.

4. Cut a pattern intermediate rafter, following the RAFTER TEMPLATES, on page 88. Test-fit the rafter and make any necessary adjustments. Use the pattern rafter to mark and cut the fifteen remaining rafters.

5. Install the rafters, endnailing their top ends to the purlins and toenailing their bottom ends to the beams with 16d nails. Install metal anchors to secure the bottom rafter ends to the beams.

Step L: Install the Collar Ties

1. Cut two 2 × 6 collar ties to span between the outsides of the roof beams, as shown in the ROOF FRAMING PLAN, on page 88. Clip the top corners of the ties so they don't project above the top edges of the intermediate rafters.

2. Install the ties to the outside faces of neighboring intermediate rafters, as shown in the ROOF FRAMING PLAN—it doesn't matter which rafters you use, as long as the basic configuration matches the plan. Fasten the ties with 10d facenails.

K. *Bevel-cut the ends of the purlins so they meet flush with the rafter faces, and install them between the hip rafters.*

L. *Install the collar ties so that the upper pair rest on top of, and are perpendicular to, the lower pair.*

M. *Miter the ends of the sheathing boards and make sure the tongue-and-groove joints are tight before nailing.*

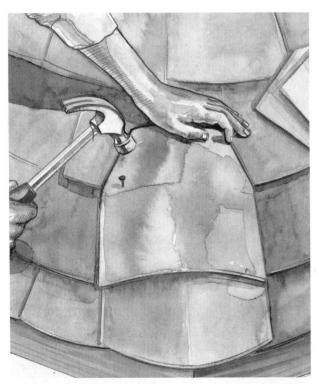

N. *Shingle the roof sides individually, then cover the hip ridges with caps, overlapping the shingles equally on both sides.*

3. Set two uncut 2 × 6 collar ties on top of—and perpendicular to—the installed collar ties so both ends extend beyond the intermediate rafters on opposing sides of the roof (see the ROOF FRAMING PLAN, on page 88). Mark the ends of the ties by tracing along the top rafter edges.

4. Cut the marked ties, then clip the top corners. Fasten the ties to the outside faces of the rafters with 10d nails.

Step M: Add the Fascia & Roof Sheathing

1. Cut the 2 × 4 fascia, mitering the ends at 22½°. Install the fascia with its top edges ¾" above the rafters so it will be flush with the roof sheathing—use 16d galv. casing nails.

2. Install the 1 × 6 tongue-and-groove roof sheathing, starting at the lower edge of the roof. Angle-cut the ends of the boards at 22½°, cutting them to length so their ends break on the centers of the hip rafters. Fit the tongue-and-groove joints together, and facenail the sheathing to the hip and intermediate rafters with 8d galv. box nails.

Step N: Install the Roofing

1. Install metal drip edge along the bottom edges of the roof, angle-cutting the ends.

2. Add 15# building paper over the sheathing and drip edge. Overlap the paper at each hip by 6".

3. Install the asphalt shingles on one section of the roof at a time. Trim the shingles flush with the hip ridges.

4. Cover the hip ridges with manufactured cap shingles or caps you cut from standard shingles.

5. Piece in metal flashing around the roof hub, and seal all flashing seams and cover all exposed nail heads with roofing cement.

6. Install the wood sphere on the center of the roof hub, using a large dowel screw.

Step O: Build the Overhead Lattice Screens

1. On the side faces of each post, mark the center of the post width. Then measure over, toward the gazebo center, one-half the thickness of the lattice panels and make a second mark. Use a level to draw a plumb line, starting from the second mark and extending down 17½" from the roof beam (see the ROOF EDGE DETAIL, on page 89). Draw a level line across the post face at the end of the vertical line (at the 17½" mark). Also, snap a chalk line between the vertical lines on the underside of the beams—these will guide the placement of the top inner stops.

2. Cut a cedar 2 × 4 rail to span between each set of posts, so the bottom rail edge is on the level line

and the side face is on the plumb line—bevel the ends at 22½°. Fasten the rails to the posts with 3" deck screws.

3. Cut 5/4 × 5/4 (about 1⅛ × 1⅛" actual dimension) cedar inner stops to span between posts underneath the roof beams. Bevel the ends at 22½° and fasten the stops to the beams with 8d galv. finish nails so their side faces are flush to the chalk lines.

4. The vertical stops of the overhead screens and the screens below the railings (Step P) are 5/4 × 5/4s that have one edge beveled at 22½°. It will save time to rip all of them at once, using a table saw, if available—you'll need about 100 linear feet.

5. Cut and install the inner vertical stops with their sides flush to the plumb lines drawn on the posts.

6. Cut eight lattice panels at 16 × 39⅝". Set the panels against the inner stops and rails and fasten them with 3d galv. finish nails.

7. Cut and install the outer rails and stops to complete the screens. Fasten the rails with 3" deck screws driven through the inner rails, and fasten the stops with 8d galv. finish nails driven into the posts and beams.

Step P: Build the Railings & Lower Lattice

1. Measure up from the deck and mark the side faces of each post at 3" and 36". Draw level lines across the faces at these marks. Draw a plumb line between the level marks by finding the post center and moving inward one-half the thickness of the lattice, as you did in Step O.

2. Cut the 2 × 4 cedar top rails to fit between seven pairs of posts (skipping the two posts flanking the stairs), as shown in the DETAIL AT DECK EDGE, on page 89. Miter the rail ends at 22½° and install them with 3" deck screws so they are centered on the posts and their top faces are on the upper level lines.

3. Cut and install the 2 × 4 inner bottom rails and 5/4 × 5/4 stops, following the procedure in Step O.

4. Cut the lattice panels at 31 × 39⅝". Fasten the panels against the stops and lower rails with 3d galv. finish nails.

5. Cut and install the outer bottom rails, securing them with screws, then cut and install the outer horizontal and vertical stops.

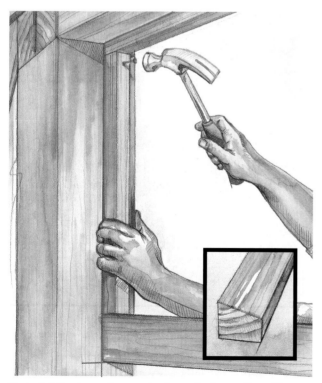

O. *Install the inner stops and rails on the layout lines. The vertical stops are beveled at 22½° (inset).*

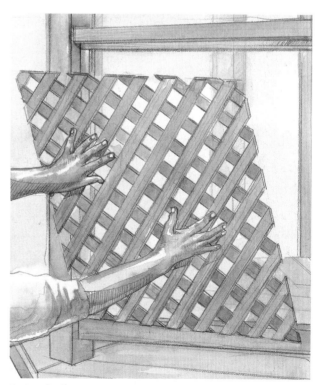

P. *Set the lattice panels against the inner stops and rails, and fasten them with 3d galvanized finish nails.*

Playhouse

This 7½ × 8-ft. playhouse has many of the architectural details you'll find on a real house, making it a truly special place for play—and a fun project to build. With two homemade windows and a door-window, the 5 × 8-ft. interior of the main house is a bright but private space. Outside, a 2½-ft.-deep covered porch provides additional shelter for playing, lounging, or welcoming guests. The entire building is supported by a single floor frame attached to a wooden skid foundation, which helps make the playhouse easy to move.

As shown, the playhouse is a complete building, ready for play, but its simple design leaves plenty of room for you and your children to do some of your own decorating. For starters, the plan suggests the option of finishing the house interior with ¼" prefinished plywood paneling. You can also finish the ceiling by installing a few extra collar ties between the rafters and paneling over the roof frame.

For decorations and hardware, look through some home accessory and restoration catalogs—they're full of decorative curiosities and interesting replica pieces perfect for adding charm to a little house.

Materials

Description	Quantity/Size	Material
Foundation		
Drainage material	1 cu. yd.	Compactible gravel
Skids	3 @ 8'-0"	4 × 4 treated timbers
Floor Framing		
Rim joists	2 @ 8'-0"	2 × 6 pressure-treated
Joists	7 @ 8'-0"	2 × 6 pressure-treated
Joist clip angles	14	3" × 3" × 3" × 16-gauge galvanized
Floor sheathing	2 sheets @ 4 × 8'	¾" tongue-and-groove/ exterior-grade plywood
Decking	6 @ 9'-0"	1 × 6 pressure-treated
Wall Framing		
Plates	4 @ 8'-0", 4 @ 6'-0"	2 × 4
Studs	32 @ 6'-0", 2 @ 8'-0"	2 × 4
Headers	3 @ 6'-0"	2 × 6
Header spacers	3 @ 3'-0"	½" plywood—5" wide
Misc. framing	4 @ 10'-0"	2 × 4
Sheathing	7 sheets @ 4 × 8'	½" ext.-grade plywood
Interior paneling (optional)	7 sheets @ 4 × 8'	¼" plywood paneling
Porch Framing		
Posts	2 @ 5'-0"	4 × 4 cedar
Beam	1 @ 10'-0"	4 × 6 cedar
Post bases	2, with nails	Simpson BC40
Post/beam caps	2, with nails	Simpson BC4
Roof Framing		
Rafters	16 @ 8'-0"	2 × 4
Metal anchors—rafters	23, with nails	Simpson H2.5
Rafter straps	8 @ 12"-long	Simpson LSTA
Ridge board	1 @ 10'-0"	2 × 6
Lookouts	1 @ 6-0"	2 × 4
Collar ties	1 @ 8'-0"	2 × 4
Roofing		
Roof sheathing	4 sheets @ 4 × 8'	½" ext.-grade plywood
Shingles	100 sq. ft.	250# per square (min.)
15# building paper	100 sq. ft.	
Metal drip edge	4 @ 10'-0"	Galvanized metal
Roof vents (optional)	2	
Exterior Finishes		
Siding	248 linear ft.	8" cedar lap siding (6" exposure)
Subfascia	2 @ 10'-0"	1 × 4 pine
Fascia	2 @ 10'-0", 3 @ 8'-0"	1 × 6 S4S cedar
Fascia trim	2 @ 10'-0", 3 @ 8'-0"	1 × 2 S4S cedar
Corner trim	8 @ 6'-0"	1 × 4 S4S cedar
Deck trim	1 @ 9'-0", 1 @ 6'-0"	1 × 6 S4S cedar

Description	Quantity/Size	Material
Exterior Finishes (cont.)		
Flashing—right side window	3'-0"	Galvanized—18-gauge
Plywood soffits	2 sheets @ 4 × 8'	⅜" cedar or fir plywood
Soffit vents	4 @ 4'-12"	Louver w/bug screen
Window		
Frame	4 @ 6'-0"	¾ × 4¼" (actual) S4S cedar
Stops	8 @ 6'-0"	1 × 2 S4S cedar
Trim	8 @ 6'-0"	1 × 3 S4S cedar
Glazing tape	40 linear ft.	
Glass	2 pieces—field measure	¼" clear, tempered
Window grid (muntins)	2 @ 6'-0"	1 × 1 S4S cedar
Door		
Frame	2 @ 5'-0", 1 @ 3'-0"	¾ × 4¼" (actual) S4S cedar
Stops	2 @ 5'-0", 1 @ 3'-0"	1 × 2 S4S cedar
Panel material	8 @ 8'-0"	1 × 6 T&G V-joint S4S cedar
Window trim	4 @ 8'-0"	1 × 3 S4S cedar
Trim	5 @ 5'-0"	1 × 3 S4S cedar
Glass	1 piece—field measure	¼" clear, tempered
Strap hinges	3	
Railings (Optional)		
Top rail	1 @ 6'-0"	2 × 4 S4S cedar
Nailers	1 @ 6'-0"	2 × 2 S4S cedar
Balusters	8 @ 3'-0"	2 × 2 S4S cedar
Fasteners		
16d galvanized common nails	3 ½ lbs.	
16d common nails	2 lbs.	
10d common nails	1 lb.	
8d galvanized box nails	1½ lbs.	
8d box nails	2½ lbs.	
8d galvanized casing nails	24 nails	
8d galvanized finish nails	½ lb.	
6d box nails	2 lbs.	
6d galvanized finish nails	½ lb	
5d siding nails	2 lbs.	
3d galvanized box nails	¼ lb.	
1½" joist hanger nails	60 nails	
⅞" galvanized roofing nails	1 lb.	
2½" deck screws	36 screws	
2" deck screws	120 screws	
1¼" wood screws	60 screws	
Construction adhesive	4 tubes	
Silicone-latex caulk	2 tubes	

FRONT FRAMING ELEVATION

RIGHT SIDE FRAMING ELEVATION

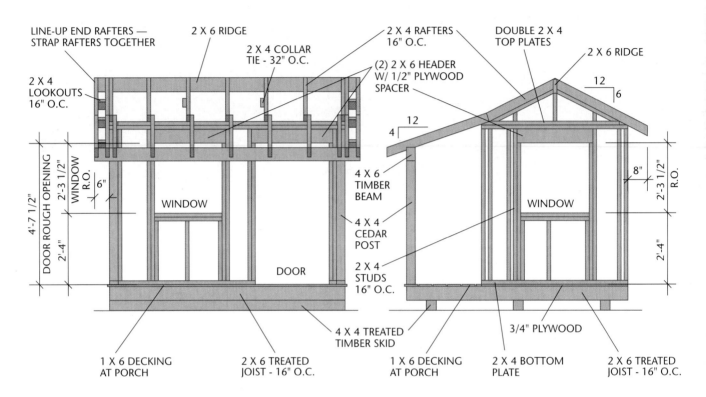

LINE-UP END RAFTERS — STRAP RAFTERS TOGETHER

2 X 6 RIDGE

2 X 4 COLLAR TIE - 32" O.C.

2 X 4 LOOKOUTS 16" O.C.

2 X 4 RAFTERS 16" O.C.

DOUBLE 2 X 4 TOP PLATES

2 X 6 RIDGE

(2) 2 X 6 HEADER W/ 1/2" PLYWOOD SPACER

12 / 6

12 / 4

4 X 6 TIMBER BEAM

4 X 4 CEDAR POST

2 X 4 STUDS 16" O.C.

WINDOW

WINDOW R.O.

DOOR ROUGH OPENING

4'-7 1/2"

2'-3 1/2"

6"

2'-4"

8"

2'-3 1/2" R.O.

2'-4"

WINDOW

DOOR

1 X 6 DECKING AT PORCH

2 X 6 TREATED JOIST - 16" O.C.

4 X 4 TREATED TIMBER SKID

1 X 6 DECKING AT PORCH

2 X 4 BOTTOM PLATE

3/4" PLYWOOD

2 X 6 TREATED JOIST - 16" O.C.

REAR FRAMING ELEVATION

LEFT SIDE FRAMING ELEVATION

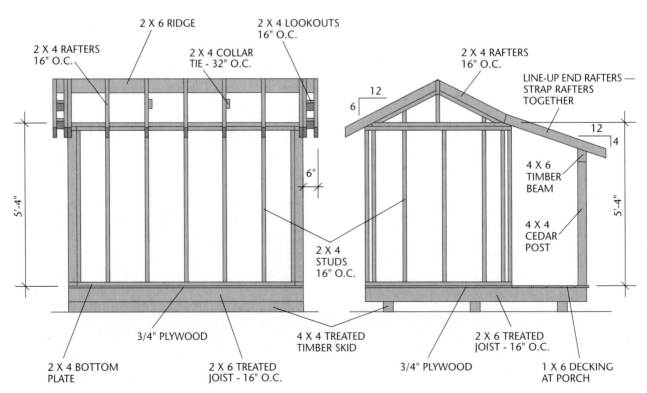

2 X 6 RIDGE

2 X 4 LOOKOUTS 16" O.C.

2 X 4 RAFTERS 16" O.C.

2 X 4 COLLAR TIE - 32" O.C.

2 X 4 RAFTERS 16" O.C.

LINE-UP END RAFTERS — STRAP RAFTERS TOGETHER

12 / 6

12 / 4

4 X 6 TIMBER BEAM

4 X 4 CEDAR POST

5'-4"

6"

5'-4"

2 X 4 STUDS 16" O.C.

2 X 4 BOTTOM PLATE

3/4" PLYWOOD

2 X 6 TREATED JOIST - 16" O.C.

4 X 4 TREATED TIMBER SKID

3/4" PLYWOOD

2 X 6 TREATED JOIST - 16" O.C.

1 X 6 DECKING AT PORCH

BUILDING SECTION

RAFTER TEMPLATES

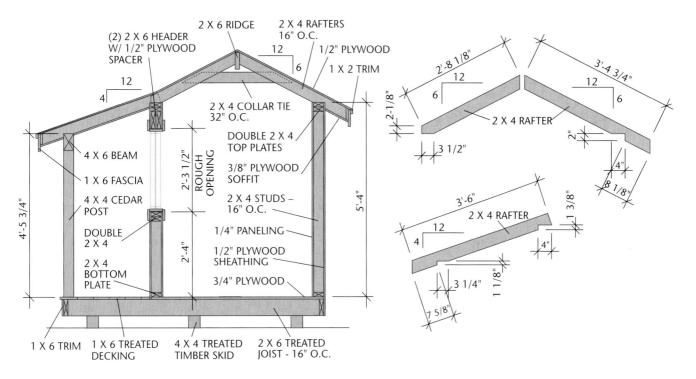

(2) 2 X 6 HEADER W/ 1/2" PLYWOOD SPACER
2 X 6 RIDGE
2 X 4 RAFTERS 16" O.C.
1/2" PLYWOOD
1 X 2 TRIM
2 X 4 COLLAR TIE 32" O.C.
DOUBLE 2 X 4 TOP PLATES
3/8" PLYWOOD SOFFIT
2 X 4 STUDS – 16" O.C.
1/4" PANELING
1/2" PLYWOOD SHEATHING
3/4" PLYWOOD
4 X 6 BEAM
1 X 6 FASCIA
4 X 4 CEDAR POST
DOUBLE 2 X 4
2 X 4 BOTTOM PLATE
2'-3 1/2" ROUGH OPENING
2'-4"
4'-5 3/4"
5'-4"
12 / 4
12 / 6

1 X 6 TRIM
1 X 6 TREATED DECKING
4 X 4 TREATED TIMBER SKID
2 X 6 TREATED JOIST - 16" O.C.

2'-8 1/8"
2-1/8"
3 1/2"
12 / 6
2 X 4 RAFTER
3'-4 3/4"
12 / 6
2"
4"
8 1/8"

3'-6"
2 X 4 RAFTER
1 3/8"
12 / 4
4"
3 1/4"
1 1/8"
7 5/8"

FLOOR FRAMING PLAN

FLOOR PLAN

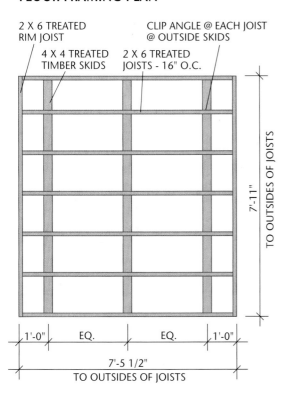

2 X 6 TREATED RIM JOIST
4 X 4 TREATED TIMBER SKIDS
2 X 6 TREATED JOISTS - 16" O.C.
CLIP ANGLE @ EACH JOIST @ OUTSIDE SKIDS

1'-0"   EQ.   EQ.   1'-0"
7'-5 1/2"
TO OUTSIDES OF JOISTS
7'-11"
TO OUTSIDES OF JOISTS

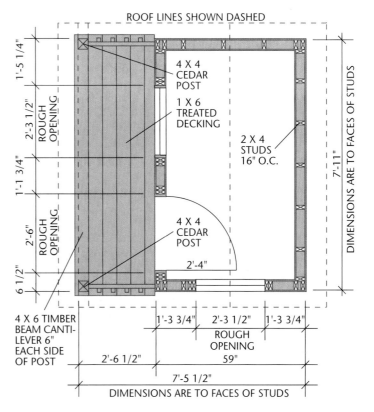

ROOF LINES SHOWN DASHED
4 X 4 CEDAR POST
1 X 6 TREATED DECKING
2 X 4 STUDS 16" O.C.
4 X 4 CEDAR POST
2'-4"
4 X 6 TIMBER BEAM CANTI-LEVER 6" EACH SIDE OF POST

1'-5 1/4"
2'-3 1/2" ROUGH OPENING
1'-1 3/4"
2'-6" ROUGH OPENING
6 1/2"

7'-11"
DIMENSIONS ARE TO FACES OF STUDS

1'-3 3/4"   2'-3 1/2"   1'-3 3/4"
ROUGH OPENING 59"
2'-6 1/2"
7'-5 1/2"
DIMENSIONS ARE TO FACES OF STUDS

101

FRONT ELEVATION

1 X 2 TRIM   1 X 3 TRIM   ASPHALT SHINGLES

LEFT SIDE ELEVATION

4 X 6 TIMBER BEAM   1 X 3 TRIM   1 X 2 TRIM

1 X 4 TRIM   FLASHING

1 X 6 FASCIA

4 X 4 CEDAR POST

2 X 4/2 X 2 RAILING

LAP SIDING 6" EXPOSED

1 X 6 TRIM

4 X 4 TREATED TIMBER SKID   1 X 6 TREATED DECKING

REAR ELEVATION

ROOF VENT (OPTIONAL)   ASPHALT SHINGLES

RIGHT SIDE ELEVATION

4 X 6 TIMBER BEAM

1 X 2 TRIM

1 X 6 FASCIA

4 X 4 CEDAR POST

2 X 4/2 X 2 RAILING

LAP SIDING 6" EXPOSED

1 X 4 TRIM

4 X 4 TREATED TIMBER SKID   1 X 6 TREATED DECKING   1 X 6 TRIM

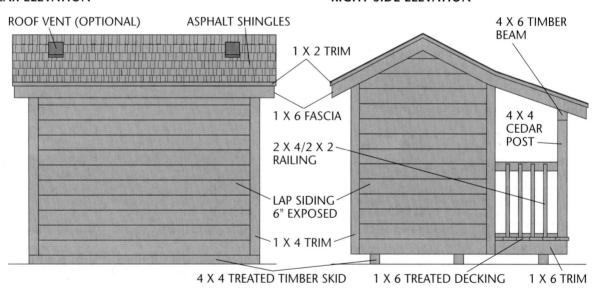

DOOR ELEVATIONS

2'-4"

1 X 3 TRIM MITER CORNERS

GLASS

A — A

4'-6"

1 X 6 T&G V-JT. BOARDS HORIZ. - GLUE & SCREW TO OUTSIDE BOARDS

INSIDE ELEVATION

6"   1'-4"   6"

R.O.

6"

1'-6"   R.O.

GLASS

A — A

1 X 3 TRIM MITER CORNERS

HINGE

1 X 6 T&G V-JT. BOARDS VERTICAL

OUTSIDE ELEVATION

6"

1 X 3 TRIM (INSIDE)

GLASS

1 X STOP RIP TO FIT

1 X 3 TRIM (OUTSIDE)

DOOR PANELS

SECTION A-A

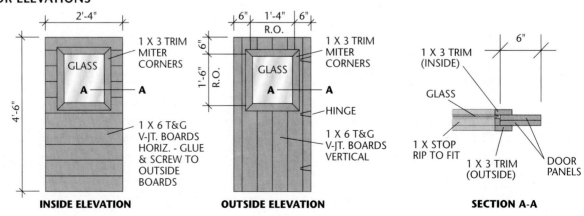

EAVE DETAIL (REAR)

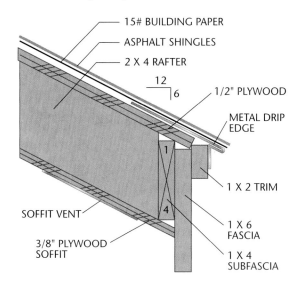

15# BUILDING PAPER

ASPHALT SHINGLES

2 X 4 RAFTER

12
6

1/2" PLYWOOD

METAL DRIP EDGE

1 X 2 TRIM

1 X 6 FASCIA

1 X 4 SUBFASCIA

SOFFIT VENT

3/8" PLYWOOD SOFFIT

GABLE OVERHANG DETAIL

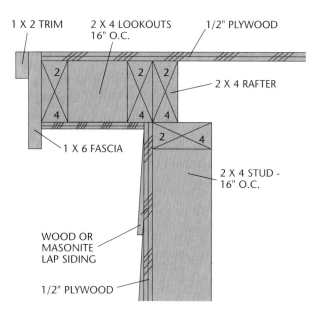

1 X 2 TRIM

2 X 4 LOOKOUTS 16" O.C.

1/2" PLYWOOD

2 X 4 RAFTER

1 X 6 FASCIA

2 X 4 STUD - 16" O.C.

WOOD OR MASONITE LAP SIDING

1/2" PLYWOOD

WINDOW JAMB DETAIL

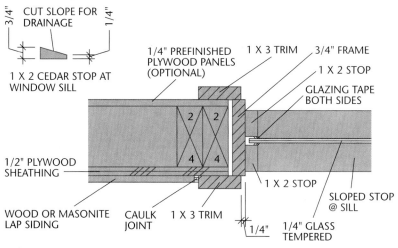

3/4"   1/4"

CUT SLOPE FOR DRAINAGE

1 X 2 CEDAR STOP AT WINDOW SILL

1/4" PREFINISHED PLYWOOD PANELS (OPTIONAL)

1 X 3 TRIM

3/4" FRAME

1 X 2 STOP

GLAZING TAPE BOTH SIDES

1/2" PLYWOOD SHEATHING

WOOD OR MASONITE LAP SIDING

CAULK JOINT

1 X 3 TRIM

1 X 2 STOP

1/4"

SLOPED STOP @ SILL

1/4" GLASS TEMPERED

RAILING SECTION

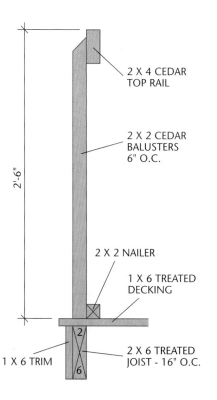

2 X 4 CEDAR TOP RAIL

2 X 2 CEDAR BALUSTERS 6" O.C.

2'-6"

2 X 2 NAILER

1 X 6 TREATED DECKING

1 X 6 TRIM

2 X 6 TREATED JOIST - 16" O.C.

DOOR JAMB DETAIL

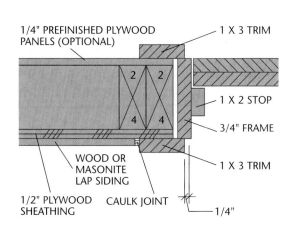

1/4" PREFINISHED PLYWOOD PANELS (OPTIONAL)

1 X 3 TRIM

1 X 2 STOP

3/4" FRAME

1 X 3 TRIM

WOOD OR MASONITE LAP SIDING

1/2" PLYWOOD SHEATHING

CAULK JOINT

1/4"

BUILDING THE PLAYHOUSE

Step A: Build the Foundation & Floor Frame

1. Excavate the building site and add a 4" layer of compactible gravel. Tamp the gravel thoroughly, making sure it is level.

2. Cut three 4 × 4 treated timber skids at 95". Arrange and level the skids on the gravel bed, following the FLOOR FRAMING PLAN, on page 101.

3. Cut two 2 × 6 rim joists at 95" and seven joists at 86½". Mark the joist layout onto the rim joists, following the plan. Assemble the frame with 16d galv. common nails—be sure to check each joist for crowning and install it with the crowned edge up.

4. Set the floor frame on top of the skids and measure the diagonals to make sure it's square. Install joist clip angles at each joist along the two outer skids, using 1½" joist hanger nails, and toenail each joist to the center skid with 16d galv. nails.

5. Cut two pieces of plywood floor sheathing at 59". Install the first piece so the groove edge is flush with an end joist and one end is flush with the rear rim joist. Rip the tongue side of the second piece to fit and install it flush to the rear rim joist and opposite end joist. Use 8d galv. box nails driven every 6" along the edges and every 12" in the field.

6. Cut six 1 × 6 decking boards at 98". Position the first board along the front edge of the floor frame so it overhangs the rim joist and both end joists by 1½".

Fasten the board with 2" deck screws.

7. Install four more deck boards, gapping between them, if desired. You'll install the sixth board after adding the wall sheathing (Step G).

Step B: Frame the Walls

1. Snap chalk lines on the floor for the wall plates.

2. Cut four side-wall plates at 59" and four front- and rear-wall plates at 88". Mark the stud layouts onto the plates following the FLOOR PLAN, on page 101.

3. Cut twenty-six studs at 59½". Cut six jack studs at 54" for the window and door frames, and cut four sills at 27½" and six cripple studs at 23½".

4. Build the headers with two 2 × 6s and ½" plywood: two at 30½" for the windows and one at 33" for the door.

5. Assemble, raise, and brace the walls one at a time, then add the double top plates.

Step C: Install the Porch Posts & Beam

1. Cut two 4 × 4 posts at 48¼". Position the posts at the front corners of the porch 1½" in from the front edge and ends of the decking. Secure each post to the floor decking and frame with a metal post base, using 16d galv. nails. Plumb the posts and install temporary cross braces to keep them in place.

2. Install a post/beam cap on top of each post, using the manufacturer-recommended nails.

3. Cut the 4 × 6 beam at 107". Set the beam on top

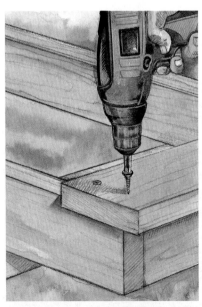

A. *Screw the first deck board along the front edge of the floor frame, over-hanging the front and sides by 1½"*

B. *Frame and raise the walls one at a time. Install the front wall flush with the edge of the plywood floor sheathing.*

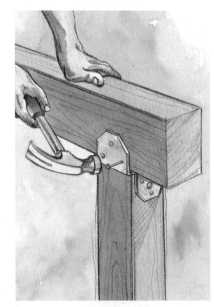

C. *Set the porch beam over the posts so it overhangs by 6" at each end, and secure the beam with nails.*

of the posts so it overhangs them 6" on each end. Measure diagonally between the posts to make sure the posts and beam are square, then fasten the beam to the post caps.

Step D: Frame the Roof

1. Cut two pattern rafters of each rafter type, following the RAFTER TEMPLATES, on page 101. Test-fit the rafters, using a 2 × 6 spacer block. Cut the remaining common rafters, so that you have a total of seven of each type. For the gable overhang, cut four porch rafters without the upper bird's mouth; cut four rear house rafters (long ones) without bird's mouths; and cut four front house rafters without the level cut on the bottom end.

2. Cut the 2 × 6 ridge board at 107". Mark the rafter layout onto the wall plates and porch beam following the FRAMING ELEVATIONS, on page 100. Lay out the ridge board so the outsides of the outer common rafters are 6" from the ends.

3. Install the common rafters and ridge board. Secure the lower ends of the rafters to the wall plates and porch beam with metal anchors. Facenail the porch rafters to the house rafters with 10d nails.

4. Cut two 2 × 4 collar ties at 39", mitering the ends at about 26°. Position the ties against the rafter pairs that fall to either side of the center rafters—make sure they are level and their ends are ½" away from the top edges of the rafters. Facenail the ties to the rafters with three 10d common nails at each end.

5. Cut the gable-wall plates to reach from the ridge to the wall plates. Install them with their outside edges flush with the outer rafters. Cut and install the gable studs, following the FRAMING ELEVATIONS, on page 100.

Step E: Build the Gable Overhangs

1. Mark and cut the front and porch overhang rafters so they meet end-to-end: Clamp an overhang rafter against an outer house rafter. Set a porch overhang rafter in position so the end overhangs the clamped rafter, using a straightedge to align it with the other porch rafters. Mark the two overhang rafters where they meet at the top and bottom edges. Draw a cutting line between the two marks, then make the cuts. Test-fit the rafters, then use them as patterns to mark and cut three more pairs of overhang rafters.

2. Cut ten 2 × 4 lookouts at 3". Endnail the lookouts to each of the inner overhang rafters and porch rafters, using 16" on-center spacing with 16d nails (see the FRAMING ELEVATIONS, on page 100 and the GABLE OVERHANG DETAIL, on page 103).

3. Facenail the inner overhang rafters to the outer common rafters with 10d nails. Butt together the ends of the porch and front rafters and join them with metal straps and 8d galv. box nails.

4. Fasten the outer overhang rafters to the ridge and lookouts. Anchor the porch rafters with straps.

D. *Install the rafters, adding anchors where they meet the front and rear house wall and the porch beam.*

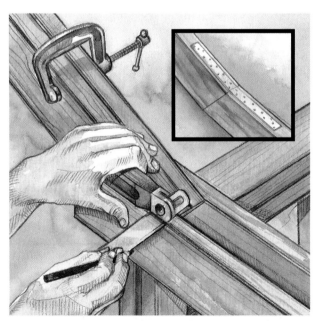

E. *Mark the gable overhang rafters for cutting so their ends can be butted together and joined with metal straps (inset).*

Step F: Install the Fascia, Sheathing & Roofing

1. Cut and install the 1 × 4 subfascia along the eaves (see the EAVE DETAIL, on page 103), using 8d box nails.

2. Install the 1 × 6 fascia and 1 × 2 fascia trim along the gable overhangs. Hold the fascia ½" above the rafters so it will be flush with the sheathing—use 6d galv. finish nails.

3. Install the fascia along the eaves, flush with the tops of the rafters, using a square or straightedge to align the fascia with the rafters. Install the 1 × 2 fascia trim so its top edge will be flush with the top of the roof sheathing. Use a square and a scrap of ½" plywood to position the trim.

4. Install the ½" plywood sheathing, using 8d box nails. At the point where the house roof meets the porch roof, make sure the sheathing joints are aligned with the rafter joints.

5. Attach metal drip edge along the eaves, then apply 15# building paper over the sheathing. Add drip edge along the gable ends, over the paper.

6. Install the asphalt shingles, starting at the eave edge. If desired, install roof vents (see page 37) on the rear side of the roof (see the REAR ELEVATION, on page 102).

Step G: Install the Wall Sheathing & Soffits

1. Install the ½" plywood wall sheathing to the framing with 6d box nails. Extend the sheathing from the bottom of the floor frame to the bottoms of the rafters, and overlap the sheets at the wall corners.

2. Rip the final decking board to fit and install it.

3. Install the ⅜" plywood soffit panels, using 3d galv. box nails. Bevel the soffit edges where they meet the fascia along the eave, at the front of the porch, at the back side of the porch beam, and wherever two panels meet.

4. Cut holes for four soffit vents. Locate one vent in each of the two outer rafter bays, along the rear eave and near the house under the porch roof. Install the soffit vents with screws.

Step H: Apply the Interior Finish (Optional), Build & Install the Windows

1. If desired, install ¼" prefinished plywood paneling over the framing, using 1" finish nails. Cut the paneling flush with the rough openings.

2. Using ¾" × 4¼" stock, cut the window frame pieces to form two 27 × 27" frames (outer dimensions). Assemble the frame with 2" deck screws.

3. Install each frame in its rough opening, using shims and 8d casing nails.

4. Cut sixteen 1 × 2 stops. Bevel the two outer sill stops as shown in the WINDOW JAMB DETAIL, on page 103. Attach the inner stops with 6d galv. finish nails. Order the glass to fit.

5. Install the glass and outer stops, applying glazing tape to the stops on both sides of the glass.

6. Cut and install the 1 × 3 window trim. Make sure the outer trim pieces are plumb and level. To create the appearance of divided window panes, build window muntin bars from 1 × 1 cedar, and attach them to the outer stops.

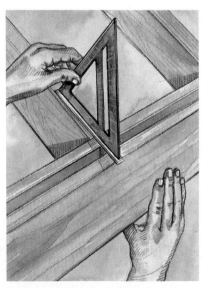

F. *Use a square or straightedge set on a rafter to position the fascia.*

G. *Add soffit vents underneath the rear eaves and beneath the porch roof.*

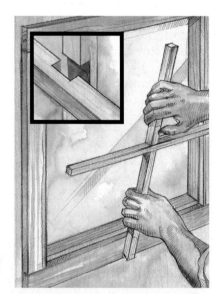

H. *Create muntins with two 1 × 1s joined with a half-lap joint (inset).*

Step I: Build & Install the Door

1. Cut the head jamb for the door frame at 29⅝" and the two side jambs at 54¼". Position the head jamb over the ends of the side jambs and fasten the pieces with 2" deck screws. Cut and install the 1 × 2 stops 1½" from the inside edges of the frame (see the DOOR JAMB DETAIL, on page 103). If you want the door to swing out, install the stops 1½" from the outside edges.

2. Cut out the bottom plate from the door rough opening. Install the frame, using shims and 8d casing nails—make sure the frame is square and plumb.

3. Cut six 1 × 6 tongue-and-groove boards at 54". Fit them together and trim the two outer boards so the total width is 28" (see the DOOR ELEVATIONS, on page 102).

4. Cut eleven pieces at 28". Fit the boards together with their ends flush, then trim the outer boards so the total length is 54".

5. Mark the rough opening for the door window onto the outside face of the door, following the DOOR ELEVATION. Glue the two sides of the door together with construction adhesive, then drive 1¼" screws through the back side. Cut out the window opening with a circular saw and handsaw.

6. Cut the 1 × 3 trim to fit around the window opening, so that it overlaps the opening by ¾". Attach the trim to the inside door face with 6d galv. finish nails. Order the glass to fit.

7. Install the glass with glazing tape on both sides, then rip-cut 1 × 3 stops to fit between the glass and the outside door face. Install the stops with 6d finish nails, then cut and install the trim on the outside face. If desired, install 1 × 1 muntins (see Step H).

8. Mount the hinges and hang the door, then install the 1 × 3 trim on both sides of the door; make sure the trim is plumb and level.

Step J: Install the Corner Trim & Siding

1. Install the 1 × 4 corner trim with 8d galv. finish nails. Hold the trim ¾" below the bottom of the floor frame and overlap the trim at the corners. Install 1 × 6 trim along the porch portion of the floor frame, as shown in the RAILING SECTION, on page 103.

2. Install flashing above the right-side window (see page 47), then install the lap siding. Start the first courses flush with the trim ends, and butt the siding ends against the trim.

3. Caulk all joints where siding meets trim.

Step K: Install the Railings (Optional)

1. Cut two 2 × 4 cedar top rails to fit between the corner trim and the porch posts. Install the rails so their outer faces are 1½" from the outsides of the posts and their top edges are 30" above the porch deck—use 2½" deck screws.

2. Cut two 2 × 2 nailers between the corner trim and posts, 1½" in from the outsides of the posts—attach them to the decking with 2½" deck screws.

3. Cut eight 2 × 2 cedar balusters at 28½", beveling the top ends at 45°. Screw the balusters to the rails and nailers, maintaining even spacing between the balusters.

I. Install stops against the glass, with their edges flush with the door face.

J. Cut the lap siding to fit snugly between the trim boards.

K. Attach the balusters to the railings and nailers with 2½" deck screws.

Firewood/Garbage Shed

This versatile shed is actually two projects in one: by using the same central design, you can build a firewood shelter or a garbage and recycling bin. The differences between the two are clearly shown in the illustrations below. Both projects have four posts, a rectangular floor frame decked with 2×6s, and spaced side slats that provide ventilation. The plywood, shed-style roof is covered with cedar shingles, but you can use any type of roofing. When adapted as a garbage shed, the project includes a center post and slats on the rear wall, two posts on the front wall that define the door openings, a shelf for recycling, and three frame-and-panel cedar doors. To save on expenses, you can build the entire shed with pressure-treated lumber or use cedar only for the most visible parts.

Materials

Part	Quantity/Size—Firewood Shed	Quantity/Size—Garbage Shed	Material
Framing			
Side & end floor supports	2 @ 10'-0"	2 @ 10'-0"	2 × 4 pressure-treated
Center floor support	1 @ 8'-0"	1 @ 8'-0"	2 × 4 pressure-treated
Floor boards	3 @ 10'-0"	3 @ 10'-0"	2 × 6 pressure-treated
Corner posts	4 @ 8'-0"	4 @ 8'-0"	2 × 4 cedar
Headers	2 @ 8'-0"	2 @ 8'-0"	2 × 4 cedar
Rafters	1 @ 8'-0", 1 @ 4'-0"	1 @ 8'-0", 1 @ 4'-0"	2 × 4 cedar
Rear center post		1 @ 4'-0"	2 × 4 cedar
Door posts		1 @ 8'-0"	2 × 4 cedar
Door ledger		1 @ 8'-0"	2 × 4 cedar
Slats			
End slats	5 @ 8'-0"	5 @ 8'-0"	1 × 6 cedar
Back slats		5 @ 8'-0"	1 × 6 cedar
Roofing			
Sheathing	1 sheet @ 4 × 8'	1 sheet @ 4 × 8'	¾" CDX plywood
Roof edging	2 @ 10'-0"	2 @ 10'-0"	1 × 2 cedar
15# building paper	37 sq. ft.	37 sq. ft.	
Shingles	25 sq. ft	25 sq. ft.	18" cedar shingles
Roof cap	1 @ 8'-0"	1 @ 8'-0"	1 × 4 cedar
	1 @ 8'-0"	1 @ 8'-0"	1 × 3 cedar
Shelf & Doors			
Shelf		1 @ 24⅝ × 28⅛"	¾" ext.-grade plywood
Shelf cleats		1 @ 6'-0"	1 × 3 cedar
Door panels		1 sheet @ 4 × 8'	½" rough cedar plywood
Stiles		3 @ 8'-0" (wide doors)	1 × 4 cedar
		1 @ 10'-0" (narrow door)	
Hinges		6	Exterior hinges
Door handles		3	Exterior handles
Fasteners			
¼" × 3" lag screws	8, with washers	10, with washers	
Deck screws:			
3½"	12	12	
3"	62	62	
2½"	36	48	
2"	50	62	
1⅝"	100	160	
1¼"		16	
1"		100	
6d galvanized finish nails	30	30	
3d galvanized roofing nails	1 lb.	1 lb.	

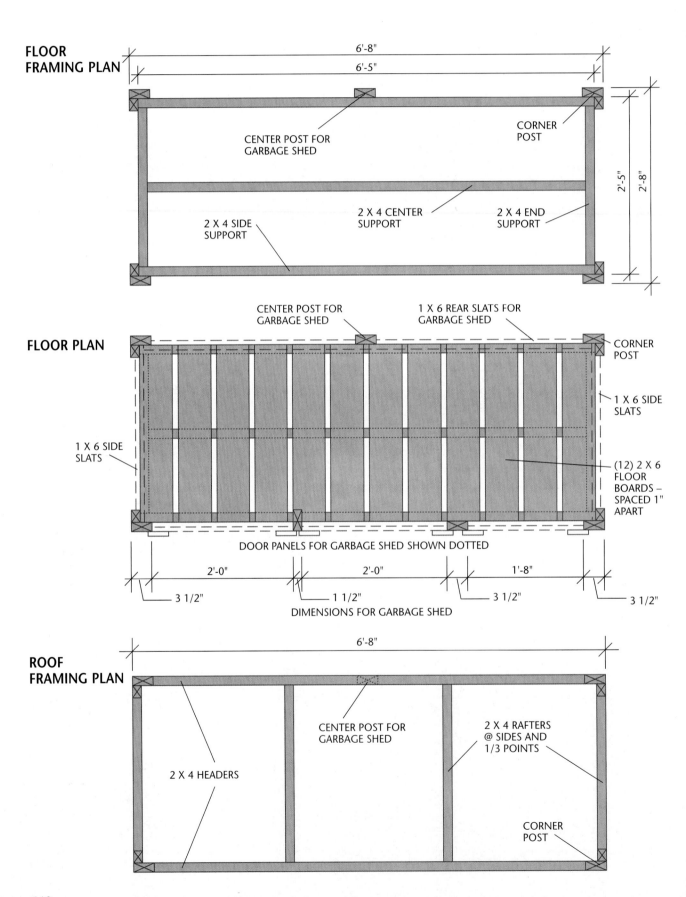

FLOOR FRAMING PLAN

6'-8"

6'-5"

CENTER POST FOR GARBAGE SHED

CORNER POST

2'-5"

2'-8"

2 X 4 CENTER SUPPORT

2 X 4 END SUPPORT

2 X 4 SIDE SUPPORT

FLOOR PLAN

CENTER POST FOR GARBAGE SHED

1 X 6 REAR SLATS FOR GARBAGE SHED

CORNER POST

1 X 6 SIDE SLATS

1 X 6 SIDE SLATS

(12) 2 X 6 FLOOR BOARDS – SPACED 1" APART

DOOR PANELS FOR GARBAGE SHED SHOWN DOTTED

2'-0"

2'-0"

1'-8"

3 1/2"

1 1/2"

3 1/2"

3 1/2"

DIMENSIONS FOR GARBAGE SHED

ROOF FRAMING PLAN

6'-8"

CENTER POST FOR GARBAGE SHED

2 X 4 RAFTERS @ SIDES AND 1/3 POINTS

2 X 4 HEADERS

CORNER POST

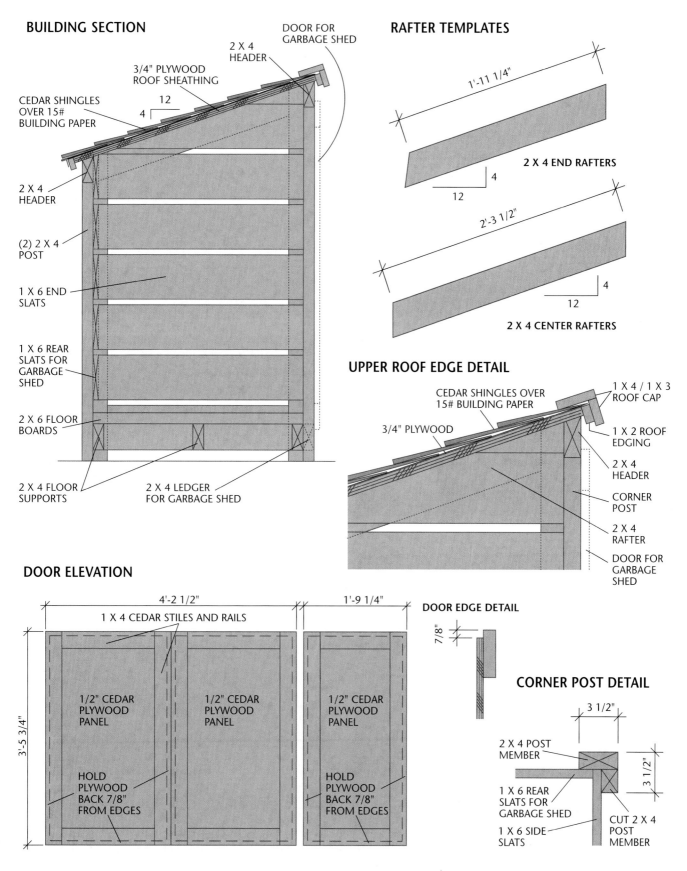

BUILDING SECTION

DOOR FOR GARBAGE SHED

2 X 4 HEADER

3/4" PLYWOOD ROOF SHEATHING

12

4

CEDAR SHINGLES OVER 15# BUILDING PAPER

2 X 4 HEADER

(2) 2 X 4 POST

1 X 6 END SLATS

1 X 6 REAR SLATS FOR GARBAGE SHED

2 X 6 FLOOR BOARDS

2 X 4 FLOOR SUPPORTS

2 X 4 LEDGER FOR GARBAGE SHED

RAFTER TEMPLATES

1'-11 1/4"

4

12

2 X 4 END RAFTERS

2'-3 1/2"

4

12

2 X 4 CENTER RAFTERS

UPPER ROOF EDGE DETAIL

CEDAR SHINGLES OVER 15# BUILDING PAPER

3/4" PLYWOOD

1 X 4 / 1 X 3 ROOF CAP

1 X 2 ROOF EDGING

2 X 4 HEADER

CORNER POST

2 X 4 RAFTER

DOOR FOR GARBAGE SHED

DOOR ELEVATION

4'-2 1/2"

1'-9 1/4"

1 X 4 CEDAR STILES AND RAILS

3'-5 3/4"

1/2" CEDAR PLYWOOD PANEL

1/2" CEDAR PLYWOOD PANEL

1/2" CEDAR PLYWOOD PANEL

HOLD PLYWOOD BACK 7/8" FROM EDGES

HOLD PLYWOOD BACK 7/8" FROM EDGES

DOOR EDGE DETAIL

7/8"

CORNER POST DETAIL

3 1/2"

2 X 4 POST MEMBER

3 1/2"

1 X 6 REAR SLATS FOR GARBAGE SHED

1 X 6 SIDE SLATS

CUT 2 X 4 POST MEMBER

FRONT ELEVATION

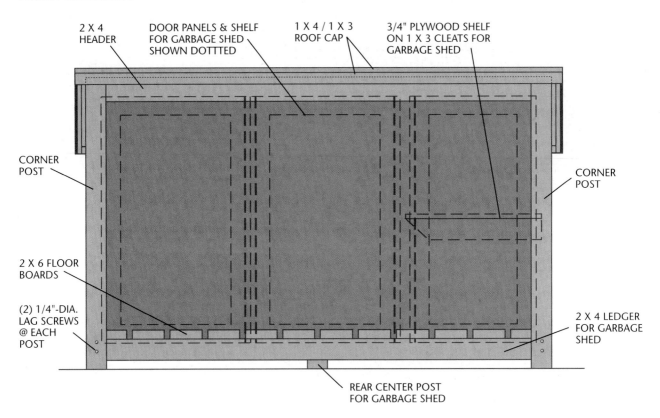

2 X 4 HEADER

DOOR PANELS & SHELF FOR GARBAGE SHED SHOWN DOTTTED

1 X 4 / 1 X 3 ROOF CAP

3/4" PLYWOOD SHELF ON 1 X 3 CLEATS FOR GARBAGE SHED

CORNER POST

CORNER POST

2 X 6 FLOOR BOARDS

(2) 1/4"-DIA. LAG SCREWS @ EACH POST

2 X 4 LEDGER FOR GARBAGE SHED

REAR CENTER POST FOR GARBAGE SHED

REAR ELEVATION

SIDE ELEVATION

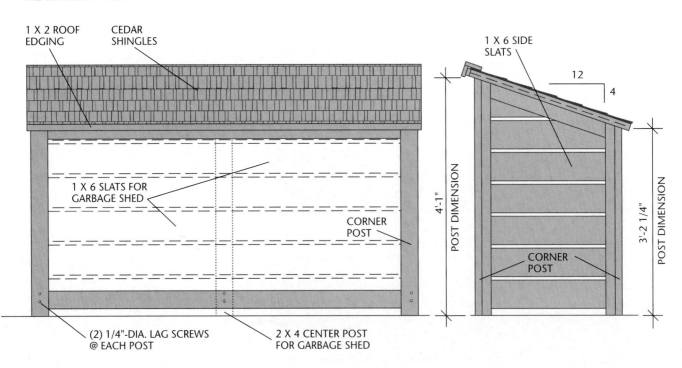

1 X 2 ROOF EDGING

CEDAR SHINGLES

1 X 6 SIDE SLATS

12

4

1 X 6 SLATS FOR GARBAGE SHED

CORNER POST

POST DIMENSION

4'-1"

3'-2 1/4"

POST DIMENSION

CORNER POST

(2) 1/4"-DIA. LAG SCREWS @ EACH POST

2 X 4 CENTER POST FOR GARBAGE SHED

BUILDING THE FIREWOOD/GARBAGE SHED
Step A: Build the Floor Frame

1. Cut the two side supports at 77" and the two end supports at 26". Cut the center support at 74".

2. Fasten the ends between the sides with 3½" deck screws driven through the sides into the ends, following the FLOOR FRAMING PLAN on page 110. Position the screws where they won't interfere with the lag screws that will anchor the corner posts to the floor frame (see the FRONT and REAR ELEVATIONS, on page 112). Fasten the center support between the ends so it's centered between the side supports.

3. Cut twelve 2 × 6 floor boards at 29". Make sure the floor frame is square by measuring diagonally from corner to corner: The frame is square when the measurements are equal. Starting at one end, place the first board flush with the side and end supports. Drill pilot holes and attach the board with 3" deck screws.

4. Cut two 1" spacers from scrap lumber and use them to install the remaining floor boards. If you are building the garbage shed, cut a 1½"-wide × 2"-deep notch for the left door post, starting 26" from the left end of the floor frame. If necessary, rip the final board so it's flush with the end support.

Step B: Build & Install the Corner Posts

Note: Each corner post is made from one full-width 2 × 4 and one 2 × 4 ripped to 2"; the boards are screwed together to form an L. The top ends of both boards are cut at an 18° angle to match the roof slope. The garbage shed also has a center post—made from a single 2 × 4—at the rear side of the frame (this is installed in Step C).

1. Rip two 8 ft.-long 2 × 4s to 2" in width. Make an 18° angled cut at about 53", leaving one 43" piece from each. Cut two full-width 2 × 4s at 53" and two at 43", beveling the top ends at 18°.

2. Assemble each front post by placing the cut edge of one 53"-long ripped board against the face of a 53" 2 × 4 so their angled ends are flush (see the FLOOR PLAN, on page 110 and the CORNER POST DETAIL, on page 111). Drill pilot holes and join the pieces with 3" deck screws driven through the full-width 2 × 4 and into the ripped piece. Assemble the two rear posts the same way.

3. Cut the posts to length with square cuts: Cut the front posts at 49", measuring from the longest point of the angled ends; cut the rear posts at 38¼", measuring from the shortest point of the angled ends.

4. Mark the insides of the posts 1½" from the ends. Position each post on the floor frame so the mark is aligned with the bottom edge of the frame. Use a framing square to make sure the post is perpendicular to the frame and clamp the post in place. Drill counterbored pilot holes for the lag screws and washers and fasten each post with two ¼" × 3" lag screws.

A. *Attach the floor boards to the frame, setting 1" gaps. For the garbage shed, cut a notch for the left door post.*

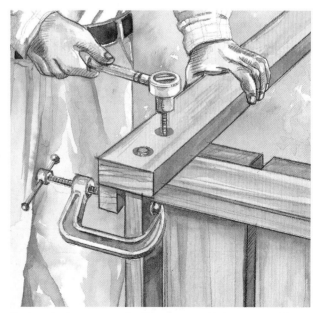

B. *Attach the posts to the floor frame with lag screws driven through pilot holes counterbored to accept the lag washers.*

Step C: Frame the Roof

1. Cut two 2 × 4 roof headers at 73". Bevel the top edge of each header at 18° (the broader face should still measure 3½" after the board is beveled).

2. Position the headers between the corner posts so their outside faces are flush with the outside post faces and their beveled edges are flush with the tops of the posts. Toescrew the headers to the posts with 2½" deck screws.

3. Cut two of each type of 2 × 4 rafters, following the RAFTER TEMPLATES, on page 111. Position the outer rafters between the corner posts so their outside faces and top edges are flush with the outsides and tops of the posts. Toescrew the rafters to the posts with 2½" deck screws.

4. Position the two inner rafters between the headers, 25" in from the outer rafters. Toescrew the rafters in place with 2½" deck screws.

5. If you're building the garbage shed, cut the 2 × 4 rear center post to length so it runs from the bottom edge of the rear header to 1½" below the bottom of the floor frame. Install the center post, centered between the corner posts; anchor the bottom end to the floor frame with lag screws, and toescrew the top end to the rear header.

Step D: Add the 1 × 6 Slats

Note: The firewood shed has slats along the ends only; the garbage shed has slats along the ends and

back side. Determining the size of the gap between slats is up to you—test your layout carefully before installing the slats.

1. On each end, cut the bottom slat to fit between the corner posts. Position the slat between the posts so its bottom edge is flush with the bottom of the floor frame and fasten it to the frame with 1⅝" deck screws.

2. Cut the remaining slats to fit between the insides of the posts. Space the slats as desired, and fasten them to the posts with 1⅝" deck screws driven through the backs of the slats and into the posts.

3. If you're building the garbage shed, install two bottom slats between the center post and the two corner posts, keeping their bottom edges flush with the floor frame. Install the remaining slats against the insides of the posts.

Step E: Install the Sheathing & Roofing

1. Cut the ¾" plywood roof sheathing at 35½ × 81½". Position the sheathing over the roof frame so it overhangs the posts by ¾" on all sides. Secure the sheathing to the posts, headers, and rafters with 2" deck screws.

2. Add 1 × 2 trim along all edges of the sheathing, mitering the ends at the corners. Fasten the trim with 6d galv. finish nails so the top edges are flush with the plywood.

3. Apply 15# building paper to the sheathing and

C. *Fasten the outer rafters between the posts with screws. Drive two screws on the inside face and one at the bottom.*

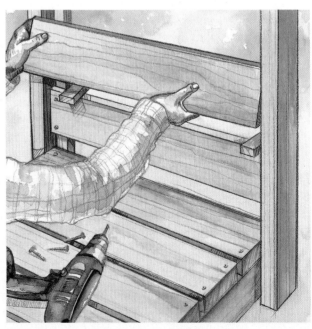

D. *Attach the end slats to the inside faces of the corner posts. Set consistent gaps between all of the slats.*

edging. Overhang the bottom edge by 1" and the sides by ½". Install the cedar shingles.

4. Build the roof cap from a cedar 1 × 3 and 1 × 4. Cut both pieces to span the length of the roof along the front edge. Set the 1 × 4 over the edge of the 1 × 3 and nail them together with 6d galvanized finish nails.

Note: If you're building the firewood shed, you have finished. If you're building the garbage shed, you have two more steps to go.

Step F: Complete the Garbage Shed Framing

1. Cut the 2 × 4 door ledger at 73". Position the ledger between the front corner posts so its top edge is flush with the top edge of the side support of the floor frame. Fasten the ledger with 2½" deck screws driven through the side support and into the ledger.

2. Cut the 2 × 4 door posts to fit between the ledger and the front header. Position the door posts following the FLOOR FRAMING PLAN on page 110 (note that the left post is on-edge and the right post is flat). Make sure the posts are plumb, and fasten them with 2½" deck screws.

Step G: Add the Shelf & Doors

1. Mark the positions of the shelf cleats onto the inside faces of the rear, side and end slats and the right door post. Measure up from the shed floor and make marks at 17".

2. Cut the 1 × 3 shelf cleats, one each at 26½", 24½", and 3½". Position the cleats with their top edges on the 17" height marks, and fasten them to the slats and post with 1¼" deck screws.

3. Cut the ¾" plywood shelf at 24⅝ × 28⅛". Fasten the shelf to the cleats with 1⅝" deck screws.

4. Cut the 1 × 4 pieces for the door frames: From three 8-ft. 1 × 4s, cut four stiles at 41¾" and four rails at 18¼"; from one 10-ft. 1 × 4, cut two stiles at 41¾" and two rails at 14¼". Cut the door panels from ½" cedar plywood: two panels at 23½ × 40" and one panel at 19½ × 40".

5. Assemble the doors following the DOOR ELE-VATION, on page 111. To assemble each door, place the frame pieces facedown, with the rails between the stiles. Set the door panel facedown over the frame so there is ⅞" between the edge of the panel and the frame on all sides. Fasten the pieces together with 1" deck screws driven through the panel and into the frame pieces. Use a framing square to make sure the frame is square as you work.

6. Attach hinges and handles to the doors. Install the doors on the shed so they overlap the openings by ⅝" on all sides. Note: Use exterior hinges. A sash hinge with an offset that matches the thickness of the door stiles works well. To use standard strap hinges, mount the hinges on blocks attached to the door posts, so the doors can open all the way.

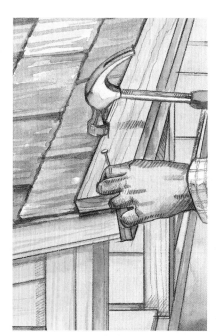

E. *Cover the shingle ends at the top edge of the roof with a 1 × roof cap.*

F. *Install the door posts flush with the door ledger and header.*

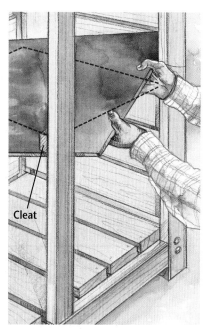

Cleat

G. *Add cleats to the door post and side and rear walls, then install the shelf.*

115

Lean-to Tool Bin

This large storage bin is a free-standing building with a wooden skid foundation that makes it easy to move. With all four sides finished, the bin can be placed anywhere, but it works best when set next to a house or garage wall (or a fence)—its steeply pitched roof and narrow profile help it blend in with the neighboring structure. The bin shown in this project includes asphalt shingle roofing, T1-11 plywood siding, and 1 × cedar trim, but you can add any type of finish to match or complement the surrounding structures.

The bin's 65"-tall double doors provide easy access to its eighteen square feet of floor space,

and its 8-ft.-tall rear wall can accommodate a set of shelves while leaving enough room below for long-handled tools.

Because the tool bin sits on the ground, in cold climates it will be subject to shifting with seasonal freeze-thaw cycles. Therefore, do not attach the tool bin to your house or any other building set on a foundation.

Materials

Description	Quantity/Size	Material	Description	Quantity/Size	Material
Foundation			**Exterior Finishes cont.**		
Drainage material	0.5 cu. yd.	Compactible gravel	Door trim	2 @ 8'-0"	1 × 10 S4S cedar
Skids	2 @ 6'-0"	4 × 4 treated timbers		2 @ 6'-0"	1 × 8 S4S cedar
Floor framing			Corner trim	6 @ 8'-0"	1 × 4 S4S cedar
Rim joists	2 @ 6'-0"	2 × 6 pressure-treated	Fascia	3 @ 6'-0"	1 × 8 S4S cedar
Joists	3 @ 8'-0"	2 × 6 pressure-treated		1 @ 6'-0"	1 × 4 S4S cedar
Floor sheathing	1 sheet @ 4 × 8'	¾" tongue-&-groove ext.-grade plywood	Bug screen	8" × 6'-0"	Fiberglass
			Doors		
Joist clip angles	4	3 × 3 × 3" × 16-gauge galvanized	Frame	3 @ 6'-0"	¾" × 3½" (actual) cedar
Wall Framing			Stops	3 @ 6'-0"	1 × 2 S4S cedar
Bottom plates	1 @ 8'-0", 2 @ 6'-0"	2 × 4	Panel material	12 @ 6'-0"	1 × 6 T&G V-joint S4S cedar
Top plates	1 @ 8'-0", 3 @ 6'-0"	2 × 4	Z-braces	2 @ 10'-0"	1 × 6 S4S cedar
Studs	14 @ 8'-0", 8 @ 6'-0"	2 × 4	Construction adhesive	1 tube	
Header	2 @ 6'-0"	2 × 6	Interior trim (optional)	3 @ 6'-0"	1 × 3 S4S cedar
Header spacer	1 piece @ 6'-0"	½" plywood—5" wide	Strap hinges	6, with screws	
Roof Framing			**Fasteners**		
Rafters	6 @ 6'-0"	2 × 6	16d galvanized common nails	3½ lbs.	
Ledger	1 @ 6'-0"	2 × 6	16d common nails	3½ lbs.	
Roofing			10d common nails	12 nails	
Roof sheathing	2 sheets @ 4 × 8'	½" ext.-grade plywood	10d galvanized casing nails	20 nails	
Shingles	30 sq. ft.	250# per square (min.)	8d galvanized box nails	½ lb.	
Roofing starter strip	7 linear ft.		8d galvanized finish nails	2 lbs.	
15# building paper	30 sq. ft.		8d common nails	24 nails	
Metal drip edge	24 linear ft.	Galvanized metal	8d box nails	½ lb.	
Roofing cement	1 tube		1½" joist hanger nails	16 nails	
Exterior Finishes			⅞" galvanized roofing nails	¼ lb.	
Plywood siding	4 sheets @ 4 × 8'	⅝" texture 1-11 plywood siding, grooves 8" O.C.	2½" deck screws	6 screws	
			1¼" wood screws	60 screws	

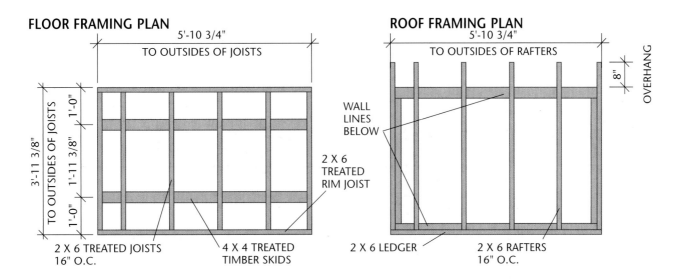

FLOOR FRAMING PLAN

5'-10 3/4"
TO OUTSIDES OF JOISTS

3'-11 3/8"
TO OUTSIDES OF JOISTS

1'-0"
1'-11 3/8"
1'-0"

2 X 6 TREATED JOISTS 16" O.C.

4 X 4 TREATED TIMBER SKIDS

2 X 6 TREATED RIM JOIST

ROOF FRAMING PLAN

5'-10 3/4"
TO OUTSIDES OF RAFTERS

8" OVERHANG

WALL LINES BELOW

2 X 6 LEDGER

2 X 6 RAFTERS 16" O.C.

FRONT FRAMING ELEVATION

REAR FRAMING ELEVATION

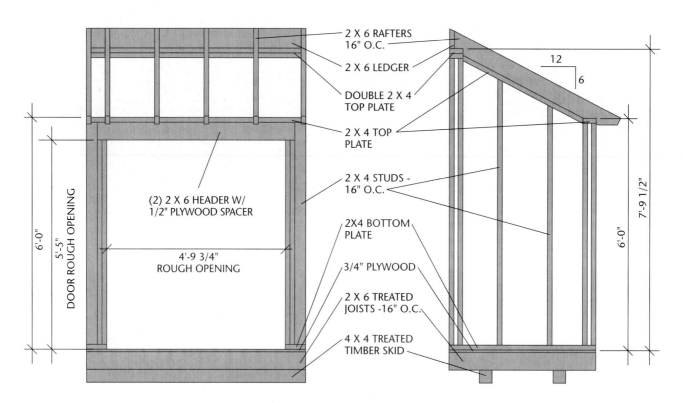

2 X 6 RAFTERS
16" O.C.

2 X 6 LEDGER

DOUBLE 2 X 4
TOP PLATE

2 X 4 TOP
PLATE

2 X 4 STUDS -
16" O.C.

2X4 BOTTOM
PLATE

3/4" PLYWOOD

2 X 6 TREATED
JOISTS -16" O.C.

4 X 4 TREATED
TIMBER SKID

(2) 2 X 6 HEADER W/
1/2" PLYWOOD SPACER

4'-9 3/4"
ROUGH OPENING

6'-0"

5'-5"
DOOR ROUGH OPENING

12

6

7'-9 1/2"

6'-0"

LEFT SIDE FRAMING ELEVATION

RIGHT SIDE FRAMING ELEVATION

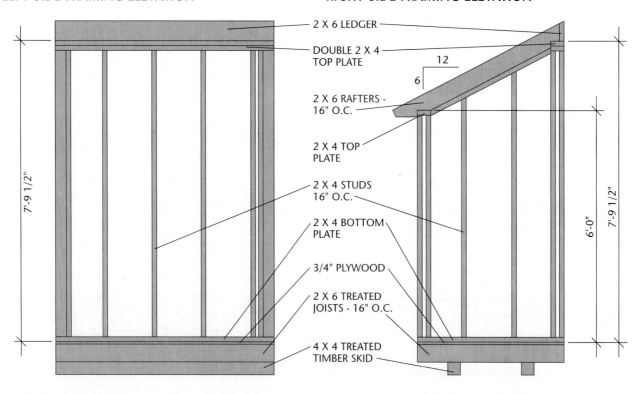

2 X 6 LEDGER

DOUBLE 2 X 4
TOP PLATE

2 X 6 RAFTERS -
16" O.C.

2 X 4 TOP
PLATE

2 X 4 STUDS
16" O.C.

2 X 4 BOTTOM
PLATE

3/4" PLYWOOD

2 X 6 TREATED
JOISTS - 16" O.C.

4 X 4 TREATED
TIMBER SKID

7'-9 1/2"

12

6

7'-9 1/2"

6'-0"

BUILDING SECTION

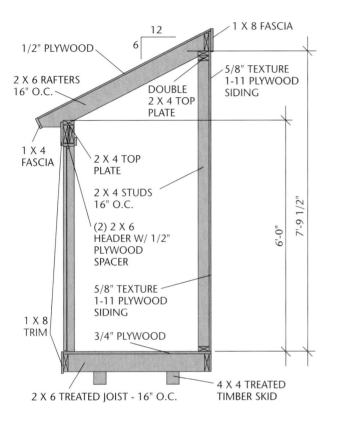

1 X 8 FASCIA

12
6

1/2" PLYWOOD

5/8" TEXTURE
1-11 PLYWOOD
SIDING

2 X 6 RAFTERS
16" O.C.

DOUBLE
2 X 4 TOP
PLATE

1 X 4
FASCIA

2 X 4 TOP
PLATE

2 X 4 STUDS
16" O.C.

(2) 2 X 6
HEADER W/ 1/2"
PLYWOOD
SPACER

5/8" TEXTURE
1-11 PLYWOOD
SIDING

6'-0"

7'-9 1/2"

1 X 8
TRIM

3/4" PLYWOOD

2 X 6 TREATED JOIST - 16" O.C.

4 X 4 TREATED
TIMBER SKID

SIDE ELEVATION

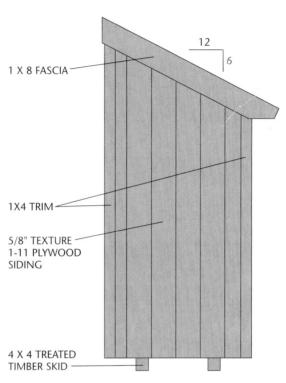

1 X 8 FASCIA

12
6

1X4 TRIM

5/8" TEXTURE
1-11 PLYWOOD
SIDING

4 X 4 TREATED
TIMBER SKID

FRONT ELEVATION

REAR ELEVATION

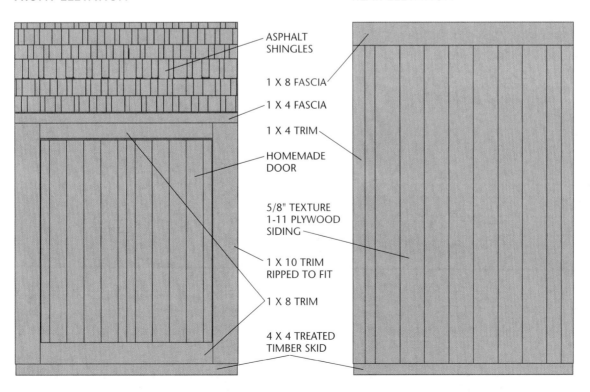

ASPHALT
SHINGLES

1 X 8 FASCIA

1 X 4 FASCIA

1 X 4 TRIM

HOMEMADE
DOOR

5/8" TEXTURE
1-11 PLYWOOD
SIDING

1 X 10 TRIM
RIPPED TO FIT

1 X 8 TRIM

4 X 4 TREATED
TIMBER SKID

FLOOR PLAN

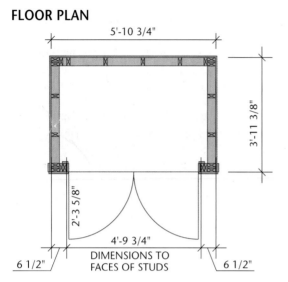

5'-10 3/4"

3'-11 3/8"

2'-3 5/8"

4'-9 3/4"

6 1/2"

6 1/2"

DIMENSIONS TO
FACES OF STUDS

RAFTER TEMPLATE

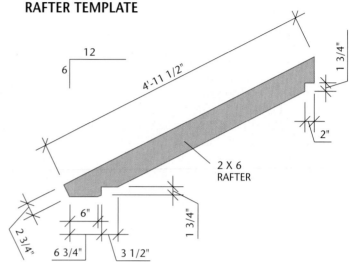

12

6

4'-11 1/2"

1 3/4"

2"

2 X 6
RAFTER

2 3/4"

6"

1 3/4"

6 3/4"

3 1/2"

SIDE ROOF EDGE DETAIL

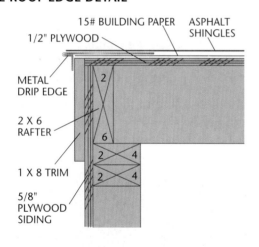

15# BUILDING PAPER

ASPHALT
SHINGLES

1/2" PLYWOOD

METAL
DRIP EDGE

2 X 6
RAFTER

1 X 8 TRIM

5/8"
PLYWOOD
SIDING

OVERHANG DETAIL

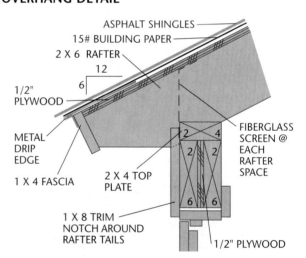

ASPHALT SHINGLES

15# BUILDING PAPER

2 X 6 RAFTER

12

6

1/2"
PLYWOOD

METAL
DRIP
EDGE

1 X 4 FASCIA

2 X 4 TOP
PLATE

1 X 8 TRIM
NOTCH AROUND
RAFTER TAILS

FIBERGLASS
SCREEN @
EACH
RAFTER
SPACE

1/2" PLYWOOD

DOOR JAMB DETAIL

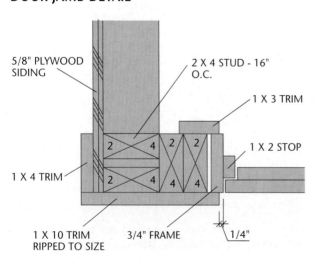

5/8" PLYWOOD
SIDING

2 X 4 STUD - 16"
O.C.

1 X 3 TRIM

1 X 2 STOP

1 X 4 TRIM

1 X 10 TRIM
RIPPED TO SIZE

3/4" FRAME

1/4"

DOOR ELEVATIONS

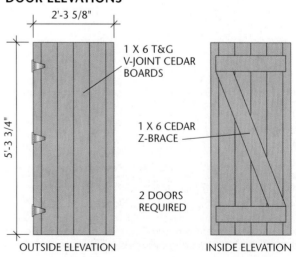

2'-3 5/8"

5'-3 3/4"

1 X 6 T&G
V-JOINT CEDAR
BOARDS

1 X 6 CEDAR
Z-BRACE

2 DOORS
REQUIRED

OUTSIDE ELEVATION

INSIDE ELEVATION

BUILDING THE LEAN-TO TOOL BIN

Step A: Build the Foundation & Floor Frame

1. Excavate the building site and add a 4" layer of compactible gravel. Tamp the gravel thoroughly, making sure it is flat and level.

2. Cut two 4 × 4 treated timber skids at 70¾". Arrange and level the skids on the gravel bed, following the FLOOR FRAMING PLAN, on page 117.

3. Cut two 2 × 6 rim joists at 70¾", and cut six joists at 44⅜". Mark the joist layout onto the rim joists, following the plan. Assemble the frame with 16d galv. common nails—be sure to check each joist for crowning and to install it with the crowned edge up.

4. Set the floor frame on top of the skids and measure the diagonals to make sure it's square. Toenail the joists to the skids with 16d galv. common nails and install metal clip angles where the two outer joists meet the skids, using 1½" joist hanger nails and 16d galv. common nails.

5. Cut the plywood floor sheathing to 47⅜ × 70¾" and install it with 8d galv. box nails driven every 6" along the edges and every 12" in the field.

Step B: Frame the Walls

Note: In this step, you'll install all of the square-cut studs and plates and the header. In step D you'll install the angle-cut studs and top plates for the side walls.

1. Snap chalk lines on the floor for the wall plates.

2. Cut the 2 × 4 bottom plates: two at 47⅜" for the side walls and two at 63¾" for the front and back walls. Cut three 2 × 4 top plates at 70¾".

3. Cut six studs at 89" for the rear wall, four at 89" and four at 69" for the side walls, and four at 63½" for the jack studs in the front wall.

4. Build the header at 63¾", using two 2 × 6s and ½" plywood.

5. Mark the stud layouts onto the plates following the FLOOR PLAN, on page 120.

6. Nail the four end studs of each side wall to the bottom plate. Raise the side walls and fasten the bottom plates to the floor. Assemble, raise, and fasten the rear and front walls, leaving the top plates off at this time. Also leave off the second stud in from the left side of the rear wall (toenail that stud in place after nailing the corners together). Nail together the corner studs of the adjacent walls, making sure the studs are plumb.

7. Install the rear top plates, one at a time—the plates should span between the outsides of the side-wall studs. Install the single top plate on the front wall, making sure the door opening is square.

A. *Check the squareness of the floor frame by measuring diagonally between the outsides of the corners.*

B. *Install the front and rear top plates so they span the width of building, covering the side-wall end studs.*

Step C: Frame the Roof

1. Cut six 2 × 6 rafters, following the RAFTER TEMPLATE, on page 120.

2. Cut the 2 × 6 ledger at 70¾" and rip it down to 4⁵⁄₁₆" in overall width, cutting a 26½° bevel along the top edge. Mark the rafter layout onto the front face of the ledger and the top plate of the front wall, following the ROOF FRAMING PLAN, on page 117.

3. Position the ledger on the rear wall, so its outside face is flush with the outside of the wall and its ends are flush with the outsides of the side walls. Toenail the ledger to the wall plates with 10d nails.

4. Install the rafters, toenailing to the wall plates and endnailing to the ledger with 16d nails.

Step D: Complete the Side Wall Framing

1. Cut a 2 × 4 top plate to fit between the front and rear wall plates, at each side of the bin, angle-cutting the ends at 26½°. Position the plates against the undersides of the rafters so their edges are flush with the outside rafter faces. Fasten the plates to the rafters with 16d nails.

2. Use a plumb bob to transfer the stud layout marks from the bottom plates to the top plates.

3. Cut the remaining four studs to fit between the plates, angling the top ends at 26½°. Toenail the studs to the plates with 8d nails.

Step E: Install the Siding & Fascia

1. Install the plywood siding on the side and rear walls, using 8d galv. finish nails. Hold the bottom edges ½" below the floor frame, and cut the top edges flush with the tops of the rafters. Stop the siding flush with the outside face of the front wall framing, and overlap the siding at the rear corners.

2. Cut and install the 1 × 4 fascia along the front rafter ends and the 1 × 8 fascia along the rear ends, holding the boards ½" above the top edges of the rafters to account for the thickness of the roof sheathing. You can join the corner of the fascia with mitered or butted joints (for butt joints, consider from which sides of the building the butt ends of the boards will be visible). Fasten the fascia to the framing with 8d galv. finish nails.

3. Custom-cut the side 1 × 8 fascia boards. Angle the bottom ends so they are parallel to the horizontal cut of the rafters and so they taper to 3½" at the end—to meet the 1 × 4 fascia at the front. Mark and cut the rear ends to meet the rear 1 × 8 fascia.

Step F: Install the Sheathing & Roofing

1. Install the ½" plywood sheathing perpendicular to the rafters. Rip the first piece to width at about 41" and install it at the lower roof edge, then rip the upper piece to fit, and install it. Fasten the sheathing with 8d box nails driven every 6" along the

C. *Toenail the ledger to the rear wall plates, then install the rafters. Endnail through the ledger and into the rafters.*

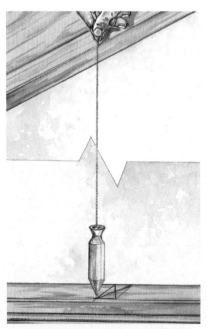

D. *Transfer the layout by holding a plumb bob on the stud markings and marking where the string hits the plate.*

E. *Mark the side fascia so it tapers with a horizontal line that meets the bottom edge of the 1 × 4 front fascia.*

edges and every 12" in the field of the sheets.

2. Attach metal drip edge along the front edge of the roof, then apply 15# building paper over the sheathing. Add drip edge along the side and rear edges, on top of the paper.

3. Install the asphalt shingles, starting at the front edge of the roof. Finish the roof along the top edge with custom-cut shingles, or install a continuous roofing strip (starter strip). Cover all exposed nail heads with roofing cement.

Step G: Build & Install the Doors

1. Cut out the bottom plate from the door opening.

2. From ¾ × 3½" (actual dimension) cedar, cut the head jamb of the door frame at 57" and the side jambs at 63⅞". Set the head jamb over the side jamb ends and fasten the pieces with 2½" deck screws.

3. Cut the 1 × 2 stops and install them ¾" from the outside edges of the frame (see the DOOR JAMB DETAIL, on page 120).

4. Install the frame in the rough opening, using shims and 10d galv. casing nails. Make sure the frame is square and plumb and the front edges of the frame are flush with the outside of the wall framing.

5. For each door, cut six pieces of 1 × 6 tongue-and-groove siding at 63¾". Fit the boards together with their ends flush, then mark the two end boards for trimming so that the total width is 27⅝".

Trim the end boards.

6. Cut the 1 × 6 Z-brace boards following the DOOR ELEVATIONS, on page 120 (keep the braces 1" away from the side edges). Lay the door on a flat surface and attach the brace boards using construction adhesive and 1¼" wood screws.

7. Install the hinges and hang the door.

Step H: Add the Trim

1. Staple fiberglass bug screen to the front wall plate and the roof sheathing, to block each rafter bay (see the OVERHANG DETAIL, on page 120).

2. Cut and install the 1 × 8 trim above the door (see the OVERHANG DETAIL), overlapping the side door jambs about ¼" on each side. Notch the top edge of the board to fit around the rafters. Fasten the trim with 8d galv. finish nails.

3. Rip two 1 × 10 vertical door trim boards to width so they will cover the 1 × 4 corner trim and about ½" of the door jamb, as shown in the DOOR JAMB DETAIL, on page 120. Cut them to length so they reach from the bottom edge of the siding to the top edge of the 1 × 8 above the door. Notch the top ends to fit around the rafters, and install the trim.

4. Cut and install a horizontal 1 × 8 bottom door trim board between the vertical boards, with its top edge flush with the floor. Install the 1 × 4 corner trim, overlapping the pieces at the rear corners.

F. Install shingle courses up to the rear edge, then finish the edge with cut shingles or a solid starter strip.

G. Fasten the horizontal Z-brace boards, then lay the angled board over them and mark it for cutting.

H. Rip the vertical door trim boards to width then notch them to fit around the rafters.

Credits & Resources

Asphalt Roofing Manufacturers Association
Phone: 202-207-0917
www.asphaltroofing.org

Cedar Shake & Shingle Bureau
Phone: 604-820-7700
www.cedarbureau.org

Certified Wood Products Council
Phone: 503-224-2205
www.certifiedwood.org

Paint Quality Institute
www.paintquality.com

Simpson Strong-Tie Co.
Phone: 1-800-999-5099
www.strongtie.com

Photography Credits

Gardensheds:
pp.2, 4-5, 48-49
651 Millcross Rd.
Lancaster, PA 17601
Phone: 717-397-5430
www.gardensheds.com

Illustration Credits

Jan-Willem Boer/
Nancy Bacher-Artist Representitive
Blaine, Mn. 55449
Jan-Willem Boer: pp. 56-59, 67-71, 78-81, 90-97, 104-107, 113-115, 121-123.

Metric Conversion Charts

CONVERTING MEASUREMENTS

To Convert:	To:	Multiply by:
Inches	Millimeters	25.4
Inches	Centimeters	2.54
Feet	Meters	0.305
Yards	Meters	0.914
Square inches	Square centimeters	6.45
Square feet	Square meters	0.093
Square yards	Square meters	0.836
Cubic inches	Cubic centimeters	16.4
Cubic feet	Cubic meters	0.0283
Cubic yards	Cubic meters	0.765
Pounds	Kilograms	0.454
Millimeters	Inches	0.039
Centimeters	Inches	0.394
Meters	Feet	3.28
Meters	Yards	1.09
Square centimeters	Square inches	0.155
Square meters	Square feet	10.8
Square meters	Square yards	1.2
Cubic centimeters	Cubic inches	0.061
Cubic meters	Cubic feet	35.3
Cubic meters	Cubic yards	1.31
Kilograms	Pounds	2.2

LUMBER DIMENSIONS

Nominal - U.S.	Actual - U.S.	Metric
1 × 2	¾ × 1½"	19 × 38 mm
1 × 3	¾ × 2½"	19 × 64 mm
1 × 4	¾ × 3½"	19 × 89 mm
1 × 6	¾ × 5½"	19 × 140 mm
1 × 7	¾ × 6¼"	19 × 159 mm
1 × 8	¾ × 7¼"	19 × 184 mm
1 × 10	¾ × 9¼"	19 × 235 mm
1 × 12	¾ × 11¼"	19 × 286 mm
2 × 2	1½ × 1½"	38 × 38 mm
2 × 3	1½ × 2½"	38 × 64 mm
2 × 4	1½ × 3½"	38 × 89 mm
2 × 6	1½ × 5½"	38 × 140 mm
2 × 8	1½ × 7¼"	38 × 184 mm
2 × 10	1½ × 9¼"	38 × 235 mm
2 × 12	1½ × 11¼"	38 × 286 mm
4 × 4	3½ × 3½"	89 × 89 mm
4 × 6	3½ × 5½"	89 × 140 mm
6 × 6	5½ × 5½"	140 × 140 mm
8 × 8	7¼ × 7¼"	184 × 184 mm

METRIC PLYWOOD

Standard Sheathing Grade	Sanded Grade
7.5 mm (5/16")	6 mm (4/17")
9.5 mm (3/8")	8 mm (5/16")
12.5 mm (1/2")	11 mm (7/16")
15.5 mm (5/8")	14 mm (9/16")
18.5 mm (3/4")	17 mm (2/3")
20.5 mm (13/16")	19 mm (3/4")
22.5 mm (7/8")	21 mm (13/16")
25.5 mm (1")	24 mm (15/16")

Index

Also from

CREATIVE PUBLISHING INTERNATIONAL

Basic Wiring & Electrical Repairs
Advanced Home Wiring
Home Plumbing Projects & Repairs
Advanced Home Plumbing
Carpentry: Remodeling
Remodeling Kitchens
Bathroom Remodeling
Flooring Projects & Techniques
Easy Wood Furniture Projects
Built-In Projects for the Home
Decorating With Paint & Wallcovering
Refinishing & Finishing Wood
Designing Your Outdoor Home
Building Your Outdoor Home
Landscape Design & Construction
Building Decks
Great Decks & Furnishings
Advanced Deck Building
Building Porches & Patios
Exterior Home Repairs & Improvements
Outdoor Wood Furnishings
Home Masonry Repairs & Projects
Stonework & Masonry Projects
Finishing Basements & Attics
Complete Guide to Painting & Decorating
Complete Guide to Home Plumbing
Complete Guide to Home Wiring
Complete Guide to Home Storage
Complete Photo Guide to Home Repair
Complete Photo Guide to Home Improvement

ISBN 0-86573-427-5 $24.95

ISBN 0-86573-592-1 $24.95

ISBN 0-86573-579-4 $24.95

ISBN 0-86573-577-8 $24.95

CREATIVE PUBLISHING INTERNATIONAL

5900 GREEN OAK DRIVE
MINNETONKA, MN 55343

WWW.CREATIVEPUB.COM

Also from

CREATIVE PUBLISHING INTERNATIONAL

Fences, Walls & Gates

*I*f you've ever wanted to build a fence, wall, or gate, this is the book for you. It's filled with practical information and clearly written instructions that lead you through projects ranging from the simple to the complex. It includes masonry walls in several varieties, including concrete block, natural stone, and glass block.

ISBN 0-86573-584-0 . . . .$16.95

Finishing Basements & Attics

*L*earn how to add new rooms to your home without adding on. This book takes you through the entire remodeling process, from assessing the unfinished space and planning the project to framing new walls and installing trim. You'll find dozens of building projects that show how to convert unused square footage into comfortable living space.

ISBN 0-86573-583-2 . . . .$16.95

CREATIVE PUBLISHING INTERNATIONAL

5900 GREEN OAK DRIVE
MINNETONKA, MN 55343

WWW.CREATIVEPUB.COM